MEDIEVAL SWORD & SHIELD

The Combat System of Royal Armouries MS I.33

PAUL WAGNER & STEPHEN HAND

PHOTOGRAPHY BY JULIAN KELSEY

Chivalry Bookshelf

Medieval Sword & Shield
The Combat System of Royal Armouries MS I.33

Paul Wagner & Stephen Hand

Published in the United States by
The Chivalry Bookshelf, 4226 Cambridge Way,
Union City, California, USA 94587
tel. 866.268.1495 (US), fax 978.418.4774.
http://www.chivalrybookshelf.com

Book Design by Brian R. Price
ISBN: 1-891448-38-2

Printed in China

Wagner, Paul (1967-)
Hand, Stephen (1964-)

Subject: Martial Arts
        Fencing | Fencing History | Germany

TABLE OF CONTENTS

From Paul Wagner:
To my father, John Wagner, who has been unfaltering in his support of myself and my family, and who taught me all the German needed to make this book possible, *warum nimst du deinen hüt nicht ab.*

From Stephen Hand:
To Karen, Lewis and Sophie, without whom this book would have been possible, but everything else in life would not.

ACKNOWLEDGMENTS

First and foremost, the authors are indebted to Dr Jeffrey Forgeng, who kindly supplied them with an early draft of his translation and without whom none of this would have been possible. The Stoccata School of Defence "Advanced" class – Luke Bonser, Charles Gallagher, Stuart McDermid, Peter Radvan, Jono Roe, Sam Spackman and Volker Stephens helped the authors with invaluable practical insights into the I.33 system. Alex Scheibner made the excellent swords and bucklers used in the photo shoot. The photos were taken by Julian Kelsey with a Canon S40 digital camera and were cleaned up by Charles Gallagher. The authors would like to thank the Anglican parish of Hunters Hill for permission to take photographs at St Mark's and All Saints Anglican Churches. The part of Walpurgis was kindly played by Zoe Tindall. Andrew Brew gave valuable assistance with German terms and Tom Leoni and Bob Charron kindly supplied translations. The book was read by Greg Mele, Brian Price, Mark Rector, Robert Holland, Linda McCollum, and Ann Price, whose constructive criticism resulted in a better end product. Brian Price is to be thanked for his design and layout. Finally, the authors would like to thank the original Priest for having the foresight to document his amazing combat system. Without him, none of us would be doing this and the world would be a much duller place.

THE AUTHORS

Paul Wagner was born in Sydney, Australia in 1967. He graduated from the University of Sydney in 1990 with honours in Biology, and studied for a Ph.D. at Macquarie University from 1993-1999. He was President of the Macquarie Dark Ages Society for most of this time, and became interested in historical fencing through his involvement in medieval reenactment. Paul studied a little bit of *Judo* and *Ju-jitsu* at school, but cannot remember any of it. He joined the Stoccata School of Defence when it was created in 1998, and has since played both a Free Scholar and Provost's prize in sword, and taught courses on Sword and Buckler, English Quarterstaff and English Longsword. He is the author of the Osprey title *Pictish Warrior AD 297-841*, contributer to *Highland Swordsmanship* from Chivalry Bookshelf, edited by Mark Rector, and is currently working on a number of projects, including *Master of Defence: The Works of George Silver* through Paladin Publishing and *Highland Broadsword* with Chivalry Bookshelf. Paul lives in Sydney, Australia, with a wife and 11 year old daughter, who is quite formidable with a staff.

THE AUTHORS

Stephen Hand was born in Tasmania, Australia in 1964 and graduated from the University of Tasmania in 1988 with first class honours in Geology. He became interested in historical fencing through his involvement in medieval and Renaissance reenactment between 1979 and 2000. Stephen also studied modern fencing between 1981 and 1987 and *Kendo* in 1985. In 1998 Stephen and two colleagues founded the Stoccata School of Defence, a school of historical fencing in Sydney, Australia. In the last four years Stephen has been invited to teach at most international Western swordsmanship events, mainly teaching George Silver and Vincentio Saviolo. He is the SSI Deputy Director in charge of publications and the editor of the SSI journal, *SPADA*. Stephen is both an Acknowledged Instructor (in English sword and Elizabethan rapier) with the International Masters at Arms Federation and a Master of Arms candidate. Stephen now works full time as a writer and teacher of historical fencing.

PUBLISHER'S FOREWORD

For many years elements of the Royal Armouries MS I.33 manuscript have been tantalizingly previewed in but a few places, its obviously complex fighting system all but lost, buried in the Latin text and within the sometimes flattened (though beautiful) watercolor illustrations.

Dr. Jeffrey L. Forgeng has been working with the RA MS I.33 for many years, endeavoring to unlock some of its secrets and bring this important manuscript--the earliest known personal combat treatise in Europe--to the attention of scholars, fencing historians, and practitioners of historical martial arts. The Chivalry Bookshelf is more than pleased to bring this important manuscript to press, working in partnership wih the Trustees of the Royal Armouries. *The Art of Medieval Swordsmanship*: *A Facsimile & Translation of Europe's Oldest Personal Combat Treatise, Royal Armouries MS I.33*, the present book's foundation, will thus offer the student of historical fencing and martial arts a critical text in a scholarly facsimile edition.

But unless one has many years to devote to the reconstruction of the system, and a substantial base in swordsmanship generally, reconstructing the system remains an daunting task. The sometimes flattened images (characteristic of the period) can make it difficult to sort out fundamental elements such as footwork, balance, and even which leg is forward for a given technique. At times this proves difficult, conspiring with the illustrations in a seemingly deliberate attempt to confound the casual reader.

Paul Wagner and Stephen Hand bring a great many years of martial arts and fencing experience to bear on the task. For five years they have worked to reconstruct the combat system encoded in the manuscript pages, making mistakes and painstakingly developing the material into a combat system that is at once effective and exceptionally complex.

Authors Wagner and Hand have succeeded, I think, in making an exceptionally complex system accessible. Their distillation of the overarching concepts and systematic presentation of the wards, their counters and the resulting plays will serve as the springboard from which many, many students of the sword will be able to extend the knowledge into the future.

Many of this book's readers will likely be experienced combatants or fencers. Those with experience in an armoured tradition, such as the Society for Creative Anachronism (SCA), Empire of Chivalry and Steel (ECS), Adria or the many European or Australian steel combat societies, will discover that I.33 is very much an unarmoured form, a seemingly civilian system that may well have applications amongst the ungentrified man-at-arms of the late 13th and 14th centuries. But even if a combatant works in an armoured tradition, the concept of the ward and counter-ward, the sloping / traverse footwork, and the sense of timing and position can be invaluable for bucklers or any other kind of larger shield.

It is my hope that through interpretative works such as this one, the rich corpus that is our medieval fighting heritage can be revived and, with luck, integrated into other allied activities.

Today the community of historical martial arts practitioners is small, but growing rapidly. Who knows, in ten years, how many thousands of individuals will be working through new fighting treatises and teaching still newer students, having built their base upon invaluable works such as this one?

Brian R. Price, *Publisher*
The Chivalry Bookshelf

CHAPTER 1
INTRODUCTION

"**Manuscript I.33**"[1] is an anonymous German *fechtbüch*,[2] or fencing/fight book, now in the collection of the Royal Armouries in Leeds, England. It is an extremely significant text, being the earliest surviving fencing treatise currently known. I.33 has been variously dated to the late 13th or very earliest 14th centuries,[3] and it presents a unique window into the world of early medieval combat.

The manuscript deals exclusively with the use of sword and buckler (a small shield gripped by a single, central handle), and while mysteries surround the text, the fencing system it describes need no longer be counted amongst them. I.33 outlines a sophisticated, complex and potent fighting style. It is also one of our few surviving texts, and certainly the most comprehensive, dealing with medieval shield use.

MS. I.33 consists of thirty-two parchment leaves, illustrated in colour on both sides. It shows a number of set plays between a Priest and a Scholar, and in the last two plates, between the Priest and a female character named Walpurgis. The illustrations are accompanied by Latin text although some technical combat terms are in German.

The characters in I.33 are illustrated wearing the typical robes of the secular clergy, and in the case of Walpurgis, the typical clothing of a well-to-do woman of the late 13th century.

Given the enormous interest today in re-creating medieval fighting, I.33 is tremendously important. Elements of the combat system of I.33 are applicable to any type of shield used. Coupled with the authors' earlier work on surviving sources for combat with the sword and large shield,[4] there is enough information for anyone engaged in sword and shield combat to make effective use of the historical techniques that our ancestors fought and died to discover and test.

Precisely what environment I.33's style was designed to be practiced in is unknown. Many techniques target the face, historically the first area to be off limits in friendly engagements with swords, so it is unlikely that the I.33 style was designed for any type of friendly or sporting encounter. I.33 also does not depict fully armoured fighting, as many of the techniques would be useless against a man in armour.[5] Apart from the manuscript itself, all contemporary images the authors have surveyed of bucklers being used in a similar style[6] show men in ordinary civilian clothing, so it is most likely that I.33 describes a system of civilian self-defence. However, its techniques are so aggressive and brutally effective that neither of the authors would think of practicing the style at speed simply wearing the robes of the illustrated participants - a Priest and a Scholar. Even in the mail shirt and open-faced helmet of a well-equipped 13th century footsoldier, all of the major target areas, including the face, would not be protected. Therefore, although no evidence exists for a military use of I.33's system, its use amongst lightly armoured troops such as archers, who often carried sword and buckler as secondary weapons, would not be unreasonable.

I.33 is a challenging text to analyse for a number of reasons. Firstly, the medieval artwork is highly stylized. The pictures are representational rather than realistic, with the distances between the figures, for example, hardly altering at all during the combat. The figures are dressed in loose, flowing robes, often making it difficult to even tell whether they are right or left foot forward. The perspective also often changes during a sequence, with the Priest on the left in one frame, and on the right in the next. The buckler often obscures hand positions, which are an important element of the style, and, then there are the occasional simple scribal errors. Probably the biggest limitation is the two-dimensionality of the illustrations. This makes the depiction of described movements such as "flee sideways" rather difficult. Yet for all these limitations, the artist shows important details. The upturned palms and reversed wrists, for example, might make the fencers appear contorted, but are deliberate attempts to represent hand positions which turn out to be highly relevant in execution of the techniques. Indeed, the authors now have considerable respect for the artist's renderings, having struggled themselves with the problems of conveying the elegance of I.33's movement style in a series of still images.

I.33 presents a sophisticated style of combat that demands expertise of its practitioners. Both cuts and thrusts are used in simultaneous co-ordination with the shield and with complex footwork, which includes passes, traverses, slips and even lunges. Like the best Renaissance rapier fencing, much of I.33's techniques require excellent point precision for the delivery of thrusts, an understanding of single-time[7] defence and the use of opposition. To fence in the I.33 style the swordsman must have the ability to co-ordinate not only footwork with bladework, but also the correct movement of the buckler around the swordarm, which is often vital to the successful execution of a particular technique. In addition, there are a number of physically demanding binding, closing and grappling techniques which are not for the faint-hearted. Lastly, a certain mental discipline is necessary to make the most of the Priest's wisdom and avoid the natural inclination to separate the sword and shield, an action which could prove fatal.

It is the purpose of this book to present the style of sword and buckler combat described by I.33 as clearly and precisely as possible, so that the modern reader may appreciate the complexity and subtlety of medieval combat. This will enable the reader to fence in the I.33 style, whether it be for sport, re-enactment, as a martial art or as stage combat.

The style will be presented in much the same order as used by the original author, a testament to the logic and system of the original work. However, while the manuscript is surprisingly logical and systematic in its presentation, it is not perfectly so, leaving some sequences unfinished, and noting some errors and omissions within itself. It is also clearly an advanced text, saying nothing of the basics of swordsmanship, and being quietly dismissive of what the anonymous author calls the "ordinary fencer." In this analysis we have endeavoured to fill some of those gaps, outlining the basic concepts and principles that I.33 treats as assumed knowledge. We have also expanded some of the sequences; for example, I.33 uses the ward "Longpoint" to demonstrate the play from various forms of "binds," and we have used those principles to complete the sequences for a variety of other wards where such binds come into play, but are not overtly explored in the manuscript itself. In such cases, we have endeavoured to point this out to the reader.

We have been working with I.33 for over five years, and have made strong and steady progress towards a thorough understanding of the work. We present the system here to the best of our current understanding, but it must be remembered that there will inevitably be evolution and revision in any interpretation. Were this book written in one, five, or twenty years time, there would be differences from the volume you hold in your hand today. We do believe, however, that such differences will be minor rather than major, and that the core of the I.33 style with sword and buckler as presented here is an accurate reconstruction of Europe's earliest systematically described martial art.

⸝ NOTES ⸜

[1] Pronounced "One-thirty-three"; the "I" is a Roman "1".

[2] *Fechtbüch* ("fencing/fight book") is the general term given to the corpus of surviving medieval fencing manuscripts.

[3] Jeffrey Singman (now Forgeng) quotes Sigrid Krämer and Hans Peter Hils who both date the manuscript to the early 14th century, although the latter quotes Alfonse Lhotsky as dating it to the late 13th. Dr Singman concludes that the text is 13th century. He does say that no one has ever published a substantial justification of any date. Jeffrey L. Singman, *The medieval swordsman: a 13th-century German fencing manuscript* in, *Royal Armouries Yearbook Volume 2 1997*, Royal Armouries Museum, Leeds.

[4] Stephen Hand and Paul Wagner, *Talhoffer's Sword and Duelling Shield Techniques as a Model for Reconstructing Early Medieval Sword and Shield Techniques*, in Stephen Hand (editor) *SPADA*, Union City, 2003, pp 72-86.

[5] Armour in the fourth quarter of the 13th and into the first quarter of the 14th centuries was dominated by *cap à pied* (head to toe) riveted mail of iron. Men-at-arms and knights added an iron casque (helmet) for the defence of the head, although this left the face relatively unguarded. There are limited references to plate augmentations for the torso and limbs, but whether these were iron or *cuirboille* (hardened leather) remains uncertain. Some combatants, particularly in France and Germany, wore closed "sugarloaf" helmets that provided protection for the entire head. Personal correspondence, Brian R. Price, May 16th 2003.

[6] Notably *Die Manessesche Liederhandschrift* of 1315 and the collection of earlier *fechtbücher* made by Jörg Wilhalm in c. 1520.

[7] A "single time" defence is a counterattack that includes a simultaneous defence, either through parrying or moving the body.

CHAPTER 2
GETTING STARTED

Figure 2.1 *The Priest's sword on the right and the Scholar's on the left.*

The primary purpose of this book is to describe the medieval combat system of I.33 in sufficient detail that it can be practiced as a modern fencing system. In order to fence using the I.33 system, whether for sport, historical re-enactment, martial arts training or for a theatrical performance, a few basics not present in the manuscript must be examined.

The Weapons

The weapons illustrated in I.33 are typical late 13th century swords and bucklers. The medieval European sword of this period was straight-bladed and two-edged, with a blade approximately 32" (81cm) long, an overall length of approximately 39" (98cm) and weighing between 2.2 and 3lb (1 to 1.35kg). The grip was only large enough for one hand, which was protected to some extent with a simple crossguard, and the weapon was balanced by a large wheel or brazil nut pommel. It was a formidable cutting weapon, with a wide, thin blade, that was stiff enough to thrust admirably when the need arose, with its sharply tapering point.

The swords shown in I.33 appear to be of Oakeshott type XII, XIII or XVI.[1] The swords used by the authors are copies of surviving originals.

The Priest's sword is an Oakeshott type XII, a very typical 13th century sword, if somewhat old-fashioned by 1300. The original, currently in the Nationalmuseet, Copenhagen in Denmark is dated between 1225 and 1275. The two-edged, broad cutting blade is 32" (81cm) long, with a single wide fuller running down three-quarters of its length. The total length is 39" (98cm), and it weighs 2lb 10oz (1.2kg), with a balance point 5" (13cm) down the blade.

19

Figure 2.2
Close up of sword hilts, Priest's sword on the right and Scholar's on the left.

The Scholar's sword is an Oakeshott type XVI, and would have been the height of fashion when the I.33 manuscript was written. The original German sword, dated between 1300 and 1325 is now held by the Royal Armouries in Leeds, England. The blade is different to the type XII in that the sword tapers to a stiff, diamond-section point, ideal for thrusting. The sword is 39.5" (1m) long, with a 33" (83cm) blade, and weighs only 2lb 5oz (1.05kg). The balance point is 5.5" (14cm) from the crossguard, which curves slightly down to allow greater freedom of wrist movement, as compared to the straight cross of the Priest's weapon.

Figure 2.3:
MSS. plate 17U LH figure showing buckler.

The buckler was a small, generally round shield with a single central grip held in the left hand. Bucklers were made entirely of steel, or constructed of wood, with an iron or steel central boss (the domed central portion of the buckler that covers the hand) and a leather or metal rim. Although all bucklers could be used as offensive weapons, some were even more effective, with spikes or spear heads mounted in the center of them, "sharp pikes 10. or 12. Inches long, where with they ment eyther to breake the swordes of

their enemies, if it hitte uppon the pike, or els sodainely to runne within them and stabbe, and thrust their Buckler with the pike, into the Face, arme, or Body of their adversay."[2]

Although the bucklers in I.33 are depicted at various sizes, they are most commonly shown as being approximately one foot (30cm) in diameter. This is the preferred diameter used by the authors. The buckler must be small enough to pass underneath the opponent's forearm in

Figure 2.4 *The face and edge of the bucklers made by Alex Scheibner.*

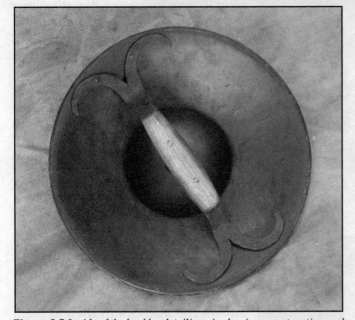

Figure 2.5 *Inside of the buckler detailing single-piece construction and handle mount.*

order to execute some of the grapples; if the buckler is much wider than a foot, this becomes physically impossible.

As shown in the photos 2.4 & 2.5, the bucklers in I.33 are not flat. They are slightly convex, raised out of a single piece of 1.6mm steel with the raising process resulting in a small spike

in the center of the buckler. They weigh about 2.2lb (1kg). The convex surface is ideally suited to deflecting strikes without jarring the arm of the defender, while the small central spike can cause considerable discomfort to an opponent. It is also worth noting that the grips are rounded and set slightly out from the back of the buckler, allowing the buckler to be gripped both face-on and edge-on as the need arises.

The swords and bucklers were made for the authors by Alex Scheibner, owner of Talerwin Forge in Rylstone, New South Wales.[3]

What to Wear

Throughout the bulk of this book the authors are illustrated wearing tunics and medieval turnshoes. The reasons for this are simple, that is what the two fencers in I.33, the Priest and the Scholar, are wearing. Why do we want to dress in 13th century clothing? Firstly and flippantly, we think it looks good and we had to wear something. Most importantly, it allows us to explore the effect of what you wear on how you fence. Modern clothing, particularly high grip modern shoes, affects the way a person moves, and this in turn affects their ability to correctly perform the historical techniques. We are certainly not suggesting that everyone fence all the time in long flowing tunics, but we do suggest that everyone fence at least once in the correct historical clothing to get an idea of how it feels and how it informs their movement. Note that we do not recommend any form of competitive play without proper safety equipment (see below).

More than any other item of clothing, shoes affect the way we move. Much medieval footwork relies on the stationary foot being able to freely rotate, which is difficult with a high-grip sports shoe. Of course we must balance this against the fact that many modern surfaces are quite slippery. Fencing in medieval turnshoes on a highly polished wooden floor is like ice-skating. Where possible we recommend wearing shoes with smooth leather soles. Many people choose to fence in old scuffed dress shoes and this works very well.

The other issue in deciding what to wear is how much armour to use. The authors feel very strongly that the most important factor in being able to safely fence in an historical style is control. Any training weapon that is the same weight as an historical sword, be it a blunt steel sword, a wooden waster[4] or a padded simulator, is capable of inflicting serious injury if used irresponsibly. It is also vital to have respect for your training partner and to never make an attack that you cannot stop if circumstances dictate. Your partner's safety must be as high a priority as your own and must always be a far higher priority than making a hit.

While armour should not be seen as being a substitute for control and for respect for your training partner, some armour is necessary for any contact fencing because nobody has perfect control of their weapon, and there are some parts of the body, such as the head and face, where even a light touch can be dangerous. Figure 2.6 shows the authors in their typical fencing equipment. The weight of the armour is not particularly great, at around 22lbs (10kg), and should make no difference to one's speed or stability when moving in the historically correct manner. Note that the primary target areas in the I.33 system are armoured. Also note that both authors are using swords with

Figure 2.6 *The authors in their practice gear. Paul Wagner, left; Stephen Hand, right.*

basket hilts. This is not correct for I.33, where the fencers use cross hilted swords, but either a basket hilt must be used, or very stout gauntlets worn (accurate replicas of 14th - 17th century plate gauntlets are recommended). This is because the hands and arm are primary targets in I.33 and they tend to be pushed into the path of incoming attacks, and hence struck harder than other parts of the body.

The equipment being worn by the authors enables *them* to fence safely. Note the emphasis on the word "them." There are some people with whom we will fence using minimal safety equipment. There are others we would not fence wearing anything short of a Tiger tank. As was suggested above, protective equipment in itself cannot guarantee safety against a two-to-three pound sword and great care must be taken to exercise proper control over any weapon.

The best way to develop the necessary control and competence with a sword or a facsimile of a sword is to be taught by a good instructor. We strongly recommend that people unfamiliar with historical fencing should train with a competent instructor rather than trying to start off by themselves. Appendix A details how and where to find instruction in historical fencing.

Stance

Like many aspects of interpreting I.33, discerning the correct stance depends very much on how much we trust the artwork. I.33 has some strange artistic conventions, such as the size of the buckler doubling when it is held with the edge towards the viewer[5] and the lack of perspective that makes it almost impossible to gauge sideways movement. Looking at illustrations in I.33 we can see two basic stances. The first is with the feet both facing forwards with the weight on the toes of both feet. Both knees are bent, with the fencer's torso leaning slightly forward and his bottom slightly sticking out to compensate. The feet are typically slightly wider than shoulder width apart. Some of the illustrations of this stance show the fencers literally on the tips of their toes, something which neither author of this volume can do. This would appear to indicate a stance where the weight is on the balls of the feet, and although this stance feels somewhat unnatural to modern feet used to high-grip footwear, supporting yourself in this manner in medieval turnshoes prevents undue slipping and allows for rapid movement in all directions.

Figure 2.7a *MSS RA I.33 plate 1U.*

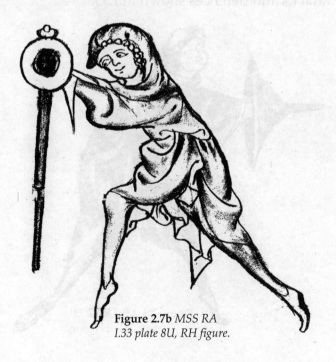

Figure 2.7b *MSS RA I.33 plate 8U, RH figure.*

A variant of the first stance shows the front foot flat and rear foot up on the toes. A second stance shows the feet at right angles with the rear foot flat and the front foot up on the toes. The spacing of the feet and the body position seem identical to the first stance. The body weight is mainly on the rear foot. The reason for the different depiction of stances in the manuscript is a matter of speculation, as common positions, such as the wards are shown using different stances.[6]

It is possible that the different stances are an attempt by the artist to convey a sense of movement or commitment of body weight. The first stance (where the rear heel is raised) might indicate forward movement, while in the second stance (where only the front heel is raised) the artist might be attempting to convey backwards movement. Alternatively the second stance may be indicating that the weight should be primarily on the rear foot, thus allowing for a particularly rapid shifting of the front foot, the first movement in many of the attacks and defences shown in I.33.

Figure 2.9 *The Second Stance (see fig. 2.10 for foot detail).*

Another factor which must be taken into account is the effect of the arm positions on the feet. If the sword and buckler are held far apart, a stance with the feet at right angles is more comfortable, while if the weapons are close together, it is more comfortable for both feet to face forwards, with the rear heel naturally raising off the ground, as in the variant to the first stance. In most cases, the authors have adopted the second stance as their preferred one, as it feels the most natural and allows for rapid movement in all directions.

Figure 2.8 *MSS RA I.33 plate 2U RH figure.*

24

Figure 2.10 *The Second Stance detail. Notice the slightly raised front heels.*

Distance

The concept of distance is critical to combat with a sword. A pair of combatants can be at three distinct ranges, *close distance*, *wide distance* and *out of distance*.[7] *Close distance* is where the combatants can strike each other without moving their feet. It is extremely dangerous to stay at this distance for more than a moment because the speed of an attack from this distance, requiring only a hand movement, is too fast to reliably defend against, and the first combatant to attack will usually hit. The correct distance from which to launch an attack, or from which to defend, is *wide distance*, where for one combatant to strike the other he must close the distance by moving

his feet. If neither combatant can strike the other with one foot movement then they are said to be *out of distance*.

A control of distance is particularly important in I.33. As will be explained later, the movement in and out of wide distance is intimately tied to the adoption of wards and counters, and thus determines the entire tempo of the fight.

It is worth pointing out that the illustrations in I.33 are often inaccurate in their depiction of distance. For reasons that are unknown - perhaps in order not to clutter details such as sword and hand alignment, or perhaps simply artistic convention - the distance between the combatants hardly changes at all, even when clearly described in the text and functionally necessary. As just one clear example, the technique called the "Shield-Knock" in I.33 is also illustrated in a couple of other sources, including the early 14th century manuscript *Die Manessesche Liederhandschrift* and Jörg Wilhalm's *fechtbüch* from c.1520. Both of these show the combatants at a distance from each other that we have found absolutely necessary for making the technique work and obeying the general principles of fencing. A comparison between these and the art-work in I.33 illustrates the limitations of relying upon the manuscript's depictions alone. Because of this, the reader will find that the photographs in this book will not always look exactly like the illustrations in I.33.

Figure 2.11 *Shield-knock from Die Manessesche Liederhandschrift (pl. 63); shield knock from Jörg Wilhalm; shield-knock from MS RA I.33, Plate 31 upper.*

Footwork

Footwork is the basis of all swordsmanship. Studying and practicing footwork is not glamorous, but we have yet to see someone become a good fencer without developing good footwork. Footwork is like the foundations of a house, not what most people look at, but without which the quality of everything else is irrelevant. Some examples of footwork are illustrated here. Practice this footwork until it becomes second nature.

If you try to swing a medieval sword using only your arm the sword feels heavy and unwieldy. Attacks with such weapons derive their power from the movement of the arm and body together. This is normally done by stepping with an attack. Thus mastering the correct footwork is absolutely critical for mastering the I.33 style.

The footwork in I.33 is not clearly spelled out as it is in this volume. Often it is difficult to gauge from the illustrations what, if any, footwork is being done or even which leg is forward. Furthermore, the lack of perspective in the illustrations may lead an unwary observer to conclude that all movement is straight forward or backward. Even "fleeing sideways" is illustrated as if the fencer moving sideways were simply moving a little back.[8] Hence the authors have to a large extent been forced to experiment with different footwork for each illustrated movement.[9] Usually this is a simple task, but at times the obvious footwork did not produce good results and more experimentation was needed, resulting in a less obvious, but more subtle and effective combination of moves. All of the footwork described here and used in reconstructing the techniques matches the text and illustrations allowing the techniques to work as described and illustrated in I.33. There are only a limited number of ways in which the feet can be moved and nothing in I.33 is radically different to the footwork found in the medieval and Renaissance corpus of texts.

All footwork used in fencing consists of passes, movements in which one foot moves past the other, and steps, in which the feet do not cross. A step or pass can be either straight (along the line between you and your opponent) or *sloped* at an angle to that line.

Terminology

While most foot movements used in fencing have precise technical names, the footwork in I.33 is not named, or even mentioned, beyond vague recommendations to advance or retreat.[10] Therefore it has been necessary, for clarity to describe footwork using terms from other sources.[11] Although I.33 is a German text, the various foot movements are necessarily given their English names,[12] as the German sources lack precise German terms.

THE FORWARD STEP

A *straight step forward* or *advance* is executed by shifting the body weight forward (by moving the hips forward, not by leaning forward), lifting the front foot and pushing forward with the back leg (this must not be done before the front foot is off the ground). The front foot is carried forward, typically about one foot (30cm) before it is placed down, on the ball (note that this is different from a modern fencing advance in which the foot is placed down heel first — if you do this in medieval shoes you may slip). The rear foot is then lifted off the ground, carried forward the same distance as the lead foot and placed down ball first. Note that the initial shift in body weight must precede the foot movement, but ideally should do so by the smallest possible fraction of time. If the foot precedes the body, the torso will lean back, making any upper body action considerably more difficult.

Figures 2.12 *A step forward.*

THE BACKWARD STEP

A *straight step backwards* or *retreat* is executed by shifting the body weight backwards, again by movement of the hips, lifting the rear foot off the ground (the heel and ball together) and pushing backwards by straightening the front leg. The rear foot is carried back, typically about one foot (30cm) before it is placed down, again with heel and ball together. The front foot is then lifted off the ground and carried backward the same distance as the rear foot.

Figure 2.13 *A step backward. The Priest moves from right to left in this series.*

THE HALF-LUNGE

The straight step forward can be used to make an attack. In this case the step should take the form of a *lunge*, although in I.33 we do not see the accentuated lunge of rapier fencers like Nicolo Giganti and Ridolfo Capo Ferro.[13] The I.33 lunge is a much more measured affair, what later fencers would have called a *half lunge*.[14] This is really just a step forward with the right foot as described above. Note that it is vital in any attack to lead with the weapon. The weapon creates a threat, while your body constitutes a target. Obviously you want to show your opponent a threat and not a target, so you must lead with the weapon and follow with the body. A more detailed examination of this principle will be made in the section on passing footwork below.

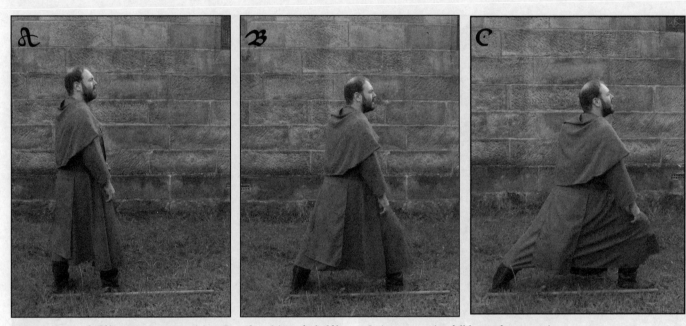

Figures 2.14 *A half lunge: A-start position, B-end position of a half lunge C-A conservative full lunge for comparison.*

From a half lunge the fencer may recover into his normal stance. He may recover either forwards or backwards. To recover backwards, the weight is shifted backwards by drawing back the head and returning the body to its upright position. As the body is drawn back, the front foot is pushed off the floor and plucked back into its former position.

To recover forwards from a lunge the weight is shifted forwards and the rear foot is brought forward on the completion of the lunge as in a step forward.

SLOPE OR OBLIQUE STEP TO THE RIGHT

Steps may also be made obliquely. The Italians called these *mezo paso obliquo*, or *slope step*.[15] A slope step may be made forward and right or forward and left. When making any step or pass towards an opponent it is critical to direct the lead foot towards the center of the opponent's body mass. Failure to do this will result in poor accuracy. Simply, your attack will tend to go in the direction your foot points, so point it at whatever you wish to hit.

Figure 2.15 *A slope step to the right.*

A slope step right is executed by shifting the body weight forward and right (as above, by moving the hips in that direction), lifting the front foot off the ground and pushing forward and right with the back leg (again, this must not be done before the front foot is off the ground). The front foot is carried forward and right and is placed down with the toe pointing towards the center of the opponent's body mass (usually this requires a rotation of about 60^0). The distance the foot is carried can vary greatly because the slope step is used to gain distance and as attacking footwork. If the slope step is used in attack, the body is not leaned as in the lunge and the distance gained will be about two-thirds of that gained in the lunge. It is useful to imagine a circle of one step's diameter around the front foot. A straight step moves the front foot to the 12 o'clock position on the circle. A slope step should move the foot approximately to the 2 o'clock position on the circle.

As with a lunge, it is possible to recover forward or backward from an attack made on a slope step. However, the recovery forward is far more common than the recovery backwards. To recover forward at the completion of a slope step, the rear foot should be lifted and moved forwards into the same relative position with respect to the front foot as before. This means that the rear foot must be rotated through the same angle as the front foot (usually around 60^0). Stepping in this way takes you off the original line between you and your opponent. Your front foot is directed at the opponent but his front foot is facing the empty space which you used to occupy.

To recover backwards from a slope step right, simply shift the weight back and left using the hips, push back by straightening the front leg and pluck back the front foot to its former position.

Figure 2.16 *Forward recovery from the right slope step.*

SLOPE STEP ⸰ TO THE LEFT SIDE

The slope step left is the mirror image of the slope step right. To accomplish a slope step left the body weight is shifted forward and left, the front foot is raised and the rear leg pushes forward and left. The front foot is carried forward and left and is placed down with the toe pointing towards the center of the opponent's body mass. Typically this will involve a rotation of about 60^0. Referring to the imaginary circle discussed above, a slope step left is made to approximately the 10 o'clock position on the circle This can seem like a very awkward foot placement, but is necessary to achieve good point accuracy.

As with the slope step right you can recover forward or backward from a slope step left. I.33 typically uses a recovery forward with a slope pace (discussed below).

To recover backward from a slope step left, simply shift the weight back and right using the hips, push back by straightening the front leg and pluck back the front foot to its former position.

Figure 2.17 *A slope step to the left.*

HALF INCARTATA · RIGHT LEG FORWARD STANCE

Another type of step used in the I.33 system is the *half incartata*. The half *incartata* is a step to the right with the left (rear) foot from a right leg forward stance, or a step to the left with the right foot from a left leg forward stance. The purpose of the half *incartata* is to take the body off the line of an attack.

To execute the half *incartata* from a right leg forward stance, the body weight is shifted to the right, and the rear foot is lifted and moved directly to the right, approximately one and a half foot lengths. The orientation of the feet should not change. The body should move sufficiently that if the right arm and weapon are held just outside the right side then the body will move from being entirely to the left of the weapon to being entirely on the right of it. Half *incartatas* are usually performed in the I.33 system immediately following a slope pace (see below). For a left leg forward stance, simply reverse all the above instructions.

Figures 2.18 *A half* incartata *from the right leg forward stance.*

33

HALF INCARTATA - LEFT LEG FORWARD STANCE

Another type of move used in the I.33 system is the half incartata. The half incartata is a step to the inside with the left foot (the Y-axis from the forward stance, or a step to the left with the right foot from a left leg forward stance. The purpose of this step is to re ... position ...

To execute the half incartata from a right leg forward stance ... right and the weight is on the right leg and move diago ... Figures 2.19 sh ... take a full ... step to the left with your right leg ... and, in so doing, turn the left of the weapon to the right so ... you are now facing the direction that the right side of ... ready to step to the off-line ... for defence first.

Figures 2.19 *A half* incartata *from the left leg forward stance.*

FORWARD PASS · RIGHT LEG FORWARD STANCE

Passes are foot movements in which one foot moves past the other, as in a normal walking motion.

A straight pass forward is executed by shifting the body weight over the ball of the front foot, lifting the rear foot heel first and bringing it straight forward past the front foot. As the rear foot passes the front foot, the latter should be rotated by pivoting on the ball. The rear foot (now the front foot) should be placed down, toe pointing forwards. The distance between the feet should be identical at the beginning and end of the pass.

Figures 2.20 *A forward pass.*

FORWARD PASS - LEFT LEG FORWARD STANCE

Figures 2.21 *Now in the left leg forward stance, the Priest passes his right foot forward, pivoting the left. He is now in the right leg forward stance.*

BACKWARD PASS ‑ LEFT LEG FORWARD STANCE

A *straight pass backward* is executed by first shifting the body weight over the ball of the rear foot. This shift will not be straight back, but will be slightly to the left if the pass is back from a right foot forward stance to a left foot forward one and slightly to the right if the pass is back from a left foot forward stance to a right foot forward one. As the body weight comes over the ball of the rear foot, the front foot should be lifted and be brought straight back past the rear foot. As the front foot passes the rear foot, the latter should be rotated by pivoting on the ball. The front foot (now the rear foot) should be placed down, heel and ball together. The distance between the feet should be identical at the beginning and end of the pass.

Figures 2.22 *From a left leg forward stance, the Priest passes backward with the left foot to a right leg forward stance.*

BACKWARD PASS - RIGHT LEG FORWARD STANCE

Figures 2.23 *Starting with the right leg forward, the Priest passes backward, returning to a left leg forward stance.*

Coordination of Hand and Foot

It was stated above that it is important in any attack to lead with the weapon (the threat) and follow with the body (the target). This is particularly true of attacks made on the pass. It is also vital that hand and foot motions in any attack be co-ordinated. While the hand holding the sword must commence the attack, it is vital for the weapon and the foot to arrive at their destination together. The sword must strike its target at the same time as the passing foot lands. Failure to do this can result in a cut that is weak, or worse, uncontrolled. It can be a little confusing to understand how you can start moving with the faster arm, then start moving the slower foot, but have both arrive together. The arm must start to move first, but its speed must be slowed to that of the foot. This coordination of motion has the benefit of allowing one to make a controlled attack which starts with the creation of a threat as well as allowing the motion of the arm to slow down, accelerate or change direction during the attack. The motion of an arm moving at full speed cannot be changed in this way. Attacking in this manner results in greater control and more options.

SLOPE PASS FORWARD ⁄ RIGHT LEG FORWARD STANCE

Just as steps can be made forward and right or forward and left, so can passes. Di Grassi named these *passo obliquo* or *slope pace*.[16] Slope paces are normally made forward and left from a right foot forward stance and forward and right from a left foot forward stance.

The slope pace forward and left in the I.33 system is typically done following a slope step forward and left with the right foot. After making a slope step forward and left, the body weight is first shifted forward and left over the ball of the right foot. The left foot is raised heel first and is moved in an arc around the right foot. As this is done the body weight must be shifted forward and left and the right foot rotated on the ball. The left foot is placed down ball first, pointing towards the center of body mass of the opponent (more detail about the exact mechanics of this foot placement and the reason behind it is contained in the next chapter). It is useful to imagine a circle of one pass' diameter around the front foot. A straight pass moves the front foot to the 12 o'clock position on the circle. A slope pace forward and left should move the foot approximately to the 10 o'clock position on the circle.

Figures 2.24
From a right leg forward stance, the Priest makes a slope step forward and left, immediately followed by a slope pace forward and left.

SLOPE PACE FORWARD · LEFT LEG FORWARD STANCE

The recovery from a slope pace left is typically forward, but may also be backward. The recovery forward may take the form of a simple recovery or a half *incartata*.

Figure 2.25 *From a right foot forward stance, the Priest executes a slope pace to the left.*

Figure 2.26 *A simple recovery forward after a slope pace forward and left from a right leg forward stance.*

To recover forward from a slope pace the body weight should continue to shift forward and left until it is over the ball of the left foot. The right foot should then be moved forward and left. It should be placed down behind the left foot, in the same relative position as the left foot was behind the right before the slope pace was made. Using the same movement the right leg can be carried behind the left leg in a half *incartata*. The right leg should be carried approximately one and a half foot lengths further forward and left than in a simple recovery forward.

Figure 2.27 *A half* incartata *after a slope pace forward and left.*

RECOVERING BACK FROM A SLOPE PACE, RIGHT LEG FORWARD STANCE

To recover back from a slope pace the body weight should be shifted back over the ball of the right foot. The left foot should be lifted heel first and should be swung back behind the right foot in an arc, while rotating on the ball of the right foot. At the end of the recovery the feet should be in identical positions to the ones they were in before the slope pace was commenced.

Figures 2.28 *A recovery backwards from a slope pace forward and left.*

Slope pace forward and left · Left leg forward stance

The slope pace to the left may also be performed from a left leg forward stance; this involves a somewhat different movement to the slope pace already discussed. From a left leg forward stance, the body weight is first shifted straight forward over the ball of the left foot. The right foot is raised heel first and is swung diagonally forward and left, across the front of the left foot. As this is done the body weight must be shifted forward and left and the left foot rotates on the ball. The right foot is placed down with heel and ball, together pointing towards the center of body mass of the opponent. The right foot should move approximately to the 10 o'clock position on an imaginary circle of one pass's diameter around the left foot. This twists the body in a manner that may seem uncomfortable at first and the left foot may remain with the heel off the ground, the body weight resting primarily on the right foot.

Figures 2.29
From a left leg forward stance, the Priest makes a slope pace forward and left.

RECOVERING FROM A SLOPE PACE, LEFT LEG FORWARD STANCE

After performing a slope pace the recovery may be forward or back. To recover forward the body weight should be shifted over the ball of the right foot, and the left heel raised (if it is not already). The left foot should be raised and moved behind the right foot in an arc. It should be placed down behind the right foot, in the same relative position as the right foot was behind the left before the slope pace was made.

To recover back from a slope pace the body weight should be shifted back over the ball of the left foot. The right foot should be lifted heel first and should be moved back behind the right foot, while rotating on the ball of the left foot. At the end of the recovery the feet should be in identical positions to the ones they were in before the slope pace was commenced.

Figure 2.30
A recovery forward from a slope pace forward and left. The back foot has simply been drawn forward to restore the right leg forward stance.

Figure 2.31
A recovery backward from a slope pace forward and left (fig 2.29). The forward foot has in this frame simply returned to its original position, yielding a left leg forward stance.

SLOPE PACE FORWARD AND RIGHT ‣ LEFT LEG FORWARD STANCE

The slope pace can be made forward and right from a left leg forward stance. The body weight is first shifted straight forward over the ball of the left foot. The right foot is raised heel first and is moved in an arc around the left foot. As this is done the body weight must be shifted forward and right and the left foot rotated on the ball. The right foot is placed down with heel and ball together pointing towards the center of body mass of the opponent. The foot should move approximately to the 2 o'clock position on an imaginary circle of one pass's diameter around the left foot.

Figures 2.32
The left leg forward stance, seen from the left. Below, a slope pace forward and right.

RECOVERING FORWARD FROM A SLOPE PACE FORWARD AND RIGHT ⁄ LEFT LEG FORWARD STANCE

As with the slope pace forward and left the recovery from a slope pace forward and right can be forward (a simple recovery or one with a half *incartata*) or backward.

To recover forward from a slope pace the body weight should continue to shift forward and right until it is over the ball of the right foot. The left foot should be raised, heel first, and moved forward and right. It should be placed down behind the right foot, in the same relative position as the right foot was behind the left before the slope pace was made.

Using the same movement the left leg can be carried behind the right leg in a half *incartata*. The left leg should be carried approximately one and a half foot lengths further forward and right than in a simple recovery forward.

Figure 2.33
A- A recovery forward from a slope pace. B- A recovery forward with a half incartata.

Recovering back from a slope pace forward and right
— left leg forward stance

To recover back from a slope pace forward and right the body weight should be shifted back over the ball of the left foot. The right foot should be lifted heel first and should be moved back behind the left foot in an arc, while rotating on the ball of the left foot. At the end of the recovery the feet should be in identical positions to the ones they were in before the slope pace was commenced.

Figure 2.34 *A recovery backwards from a slope pace, back to the original position.*

THE INCARTATA

The final footwork used in the I.33 system is the *incartata*. The half *incartata* has been mentioned above, and the two are closely related. Like the half *incartata*, the *incartata* is a movement where the heel of the rear foot leads. However, the *incartata* is a pass, where the rear foot moves past the front foot, heel first. In I.33, the *incartata* is only to throw a grappled opponent.

Figure 2.35
The left leg forward stance. In the lower frame, an incartata *from a left leg forward stance.*

Figure 2.36 *Now the right leg forward stance. In the lower frame, an* incartarta *from a right leg forward stance.*

HAND POSITIONS

Many later treatises[17] describe four main hand positions that are used in swordsmanship. I.33 does not name these. However, it is such a useful practice that the current authors have decided to name these hand positions, rather than having to describe the same hand position multiple times. In keeping with the language of this book, English names are used, rather than the usual Italian or French. The four hand positions are shown below. They are first position with the palm to the right (2.37), second position with the palm down (2.38), third position with the palm to the left (2.39) and fourth position with the palm up (2.40).

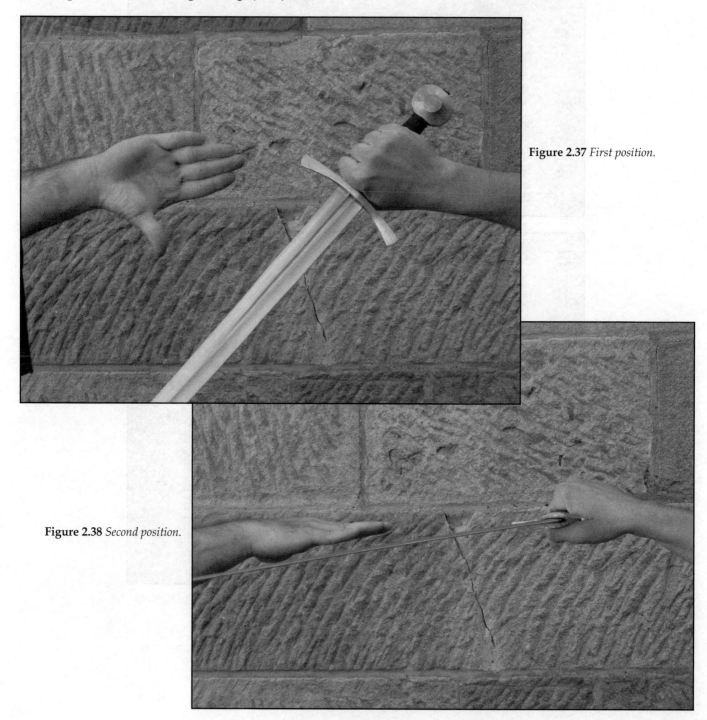

Figure 2.37 *First position.*

Figure 2.38 *Second position.*

Figure 2.39 *Third position.*

Figure 2.40 *Fourth position.*

FENCING LINE

Another useful fencing concept, not explicitly mentioned in I.33 but definitely used in its principles, is the concept of fencing line. There are four lines of attack in fencing which are characterised in relation to the position of the defender's sword hand. An attack can be launched above the defender's sword hand, in the high line, or below it, in the low line. Similarly an attack can be launched to the right of the defender's sword hand, in the outside line, or to the left of it, in the inside line. This is illustrated below.

Figure 2.41
Scholar in Half Shield from the front showing the fencing lines; Inside, Outside, High and Low.

ATTACKS

I.33 does not contain precise terminology for the direction and placement of cuts and thrusts. Unfortunately there are not any appropriate English terms for the basic attacks, so to avoid having to continuously describe cuts as "a diagonally descending cut from the right" we have decided to adopt later medieval German terminology, where the cut just described would be an *Oberhau Rechts*, or in English translation a "high cut from the right." The following diagram shows the cuts as described in the German longsword tradition that is thought to have started with Master Liechtenauer in the 14th century.[18]

The Germans did not have a terminology for thrusts. Therefore the only major thrust used in the I.33 system, the thrust called *Punta Riversa* by the Italians is referred to here as a "thrust from the left." This is the literal description of the Italian term given by Dall'Agocchie in 1572.[19] The thrust from the left ranks a close second with falling under the sword (see Chapter 3) as the most important offensive technique in I.33.

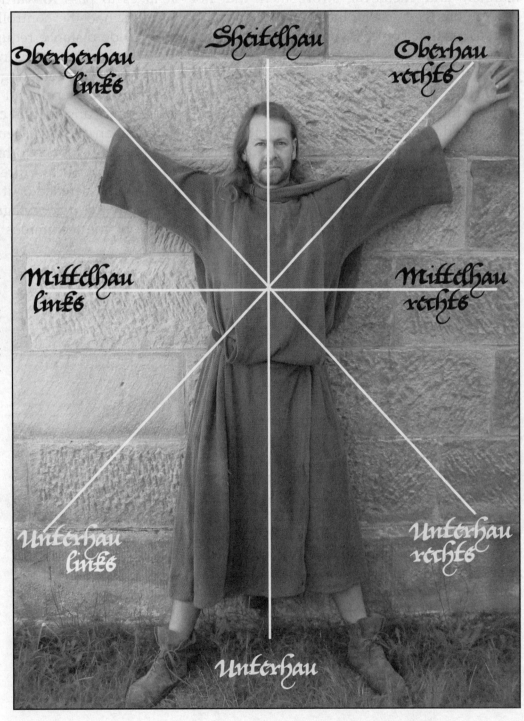

Figure 2.42
Cutting diagram using the German terminology following Johannes Liechtenauer.

HOW TO ATTACK

The medieval sword was capable of making formidable, cleaving cuts, as well as devastating thrusts. Attacks were delivered hard and fast with the full weight of the body behind them, posing a serious threat to an adversary. But the blows were not swung in an uncontrolled manner, and medieval swordsmen did not crudely bludgeon each other by hitting as hard and fast as they could. Swords were not merely steel clubs, but precision cutting weapons, and their effectiveness did not lie in percussive force alone. To cut properly, especially through armour, the sword's edge had to land truly, and the blade drawn or pulled back as it bit into the target. Swords were thus swung with an equal measure of speed and power, derived from the movement of the body and weight of the sword itself, and control and precision provided by the arm and wrist.

In preparation for an attack, a medieval sword was held in a charged position, ready to swing in with a strong cut or thrust. All of the wards shown in I.33, except for the highly defensive "Longpoint," are held in such a manner.

Attacks made from wide distance (see the section on Distance above) are timed with the movement of the feet. A typical attack might start with the sword held elevated above the head, with the left foot forward. The attacker first begins to swing the sword forward, creating a threat to the opponent. Once the sword is in motion, creating a threat, the attacker passes forward. The sword should strike its intended target at the same moment (or just before) the attacker's foot hits the ground, maximising the transfer of momentum into the weapon. The aim is to strike with the top third of the blade, around the spot on the blade that does not vibrate when the latter is struck, the *center of percussion*. This maximizes the power of the strike. It is at this moment that the swordsman begins to slide or draw his weapon, allowing the cut to slice cleanly through the target.[20]

It is worth noting that the speed of the blow is dictated by the speed of the footwork. While a sword might be swung in a fraction of the time it takes to pass forward, such a blow will be weaker than the controlled blow, and if done from wide distance requires the swordsman to step forward before swinging the arm, creating a target before creating a threat, and hence violating basic rules of timing. Because cuts must be swung in this controlled manner, the swordsman has sufficient time to redirect his weapon in response to his adversary's reaction to the attack. Such redirection may be a *feint* to deceive the defence or it may involve aborting the blow to defend against a counterattack. Many of the techniques in I.33 rely upon this fact.

HOW TO PARRY[21]

Faced with an attack as described above, the defender has several options. The first is to avoid the blow, by moving backwards or sideways. While this alone would preserve the defender, it will not bring him any closer to defeating his assailant, and so a better option is to counterattack to an open target while simultaneously avoiding the blow, either by moving aside or by blocking or deflecting with the buckler and offending with the sword. A final option is to parry the attack with the sword, and then to riposte, that is to strike after the parry.

I.33 contains a great many parries with the sword, but does not go into detail as to how these should be performed.

In the Middle Ages and early Renaissance, parries were done in many different ways, including deflecting the blow, beating it aside, or by stopping or binding it. Attacks were deflected by placing the defending blade at such an angle that the attacking blade simply slid off it, redirecting the energy of the attack away from the defender. Beats were achieved by striking the attacking blade perpendicularly to its direction of travel, to deflect it from its intended course. In the use of some weapons, such as the longsword,[22] these defences dominated, and both of them are evident in I.33.

Another category of defence was the *stop*, a direct opposition of the enemy blade. Such defences were indeed used by medieval swordsmen, but medieval treatises do not teach the student to simply stand and take the full force of a blow on their sword (as many later treatises do).[23] Instead the swordsman would close distance with the attacker by moving into the attack and crossing swords *störck-zu-störck* ("strong to strong" i.e that part of the blade closer to the hilt - see figure 2.1. Parrying with the *schwech* or weak of the sword, the part close to the point, results in a weak parry that can be overpowered by a strong

attack), choking up the blow before the attack gained a significant amount of momentum. Some of the defences in I.33 are of this sort.

Deflections and other forms of parry in which the force of the attack is not directly opposed could be done with different parts of the blade, depending on what was the most effective method for the situation. It was martial effectiveness, not any other consideration, that determined which method was used. Medieval masters sometimes specified which part of the blade should be used for a particular action, but there was no general rule, because the style of parrying did not demand that there be a general rule.[24] I.33, being the oldest known fencing manual, is typical of the earlier style. Where the authors believe it matters which part of the blade you should use, they will tell you. If it is not mentioned, then we don't think it matters.

As a final note, we would like to draw your attention to some timing aspects in the photographs of some I.33 plays. In many of the plays the first photo shows the Priest and Scholar (the authors) in their wards, the second shows an attack almost complete and the third photo shows a response to that attack. In most of these cases the photographs should not be looked upon as a strict chronological record. They are not, "the Priest does X and the Scholar responds with Y," but rather, "the Priest tries to do X, but the Scholar responds with Y, preventing him from..." In most cases the response in the third photo will be made before the position in the second photo is reached.

⸌ NOTES ⸍

[1] Medieval swords are classified according to Ewart Oakeshott's typology. This is the only sword typology the authors know of based on blade morphology, or in other words on how the sword handles and what it can be used for. It is thus enormously useful for people who actually use swords to fence with. The typology was introduced in Oakeshott's classic book, *The Sword in the Age of Chivalry*, London, 1964.

[2] John Stowe *The Annales; augmented unto the ende of this present yeere 1614 by Edmund Howes, Gent* (London, 1615) p. 896.

[3] For contact details, see the advertisement at the end of the book.

[4] "Waster" is a Renaissance English term for a wooden practice weapon.

[5] MSS I.33 Plate 1 Upper.

[6] For example the Priest is shown in Underarm in the second stance at plate 3 Upper, and in the same ward and tactical position but in the first stance on plate 5 Upper.

[7] Close and wide distance are defined in many historical fencing treatises, for example, Ridolfo Capo Ferro's *Gran Simulacro Dell'Arte E Dell'Uso Della Scherma*, Siena 1610, Capitolo IIII, p. 8-9. Out of distance is a modern term used by many fencing instructors to refer to distances greater than wide distance.

[8] For example Plate 42 Upper, in which the Scholar performs an action that can only be done if he moves a significant distance to his right.

[9] The types of foot movement used are those described in *Di Grassi His true Arte of Defence*, London 1594, in the authors' opinions the best early source for footwork.

[10] For example, in Plate 3 it is recommended that the Scholar "bind and advance." Jeffrey L. Forgeng, *The Art of Medieval Swordsmanship: A Facsimile and Translation of Europe's Oldest Personal Combat Treatise, Royal Armouries MS. I.33*, Union City, 2003, Plate 3.

[11] Primarily Di Grassi, which is as stated in note 9, the best early source for footwork.

[12] Note that in some cases the English name is actually the untranslated Italian name.

[13] Niccolo Giganti *Teatro*, Venetia, 1606, Ridolfo Capo Ferro, *Gran Simulacro Dell'Arte Edell'Uso Della Scherma*, Siena, 1610. Both authors use the word *lunga* in it's original meaning as the Italian adjective meaning long, a lunge is simply a long attack.

[14] For example William M. Gaugler, *The History of Fencing: Foundations of Modern European Swordplay*, Bangor, Maine, 1998. pp. 6 &13.

[15] Actually it literally means *slope half pace*, but Di Grassi's half pace was called a step by practically every English author. Giacomo di Grassi, *Ragione Di Adoprar Sicuramente L'Arme Si Da Offesa, Come Da Difesa*. Venetia, 1570. p.14

[16] Ibid. The words pass and pace can be used interchangeably, pace is used here because it is a specific name that appears in the historical literature.

[17] For example, Salvator Fabris, *De Lo Schermo Overo Scienza D'Arme*, Copenhagen 1606. pp.1-2.

[18] See the glossary of terms used in the Liechtenauer school that appears on pages 381-384 of Christian Tobler's *Secrets of German Medieval Swordsmanship*, Union City, 2001.

[19] Giovanni Dall'Agocchie, *Dell'Arte Di Scrimia Libri Tre*, Venetia 1572. p.8V.

[20] To cut effectively through a solid target with a straight, single-handed sword some amount of artificial cutting motion or drawing is absolutely essential. The 19th century master Allanson-Winn explained;
"A straight-bladed broad-sword requires what may be termed an artificial draw, either backward or forward, in order that a cut may have its full effect. Of course the draw back is by far the most common form of the 'draw'…if the hand retains its position throughout the entire sweep, [the edge] will meet the object to be cut simply as a *hit*, not as a *cut*. This is just what we want to avoid…No matter how extended the arm may be when commencing the cut - and the more extended the better in the case of a long, heavy sword - the 'draw' should always come in towards the end of the sweep, the first part of which is merely intended to give the required impetus to the effective portion of the cut…It is well to remember that a mere *hit* with the true edge of a straight-bladed sword is little better than a blow with a heavy stick having an oval section."
Allanson-Winn and Phillipps-Wolley, *Broadsword and Singlestick with chapters on Quarterstaff, Bayonet, Shillalah, Walking-Stick, Umbrella and Other Weapons of Self Defence*, London, 1890, p.29-32.

[21] Please note that the words *parry* and *defend* are not synonymous. Many defences in early treatises like I.33 are done by bodily avoidance and many parries are done with the buckler and not with the sword (though there is far more parrying with the sword than might be expected).

[22] The dominant weapon of late medieval fencing treatises, this is popularly known today as the "hand and a half sword".

[23] For example, Angelo Viggiani. In *Lo Schermo* (Vinetia 1575) he writes, "RODOMONTE: What parry would you use against this [*mandritto*] *fendente*? COUNT: […] When your *mandritto* falls, I would lift my sword against yours, as if forming a mandritto of my own. I would make sure that the tip of my sword does not dip, but that it stays higher than my hilt, while my arm remains well-extended. In this manner, our two swords would meet cross-wise, true-edge on true-edge. ROD. This is the common parry, taught by all Masters and used by most fencers." p. 81 translation by Tom Leoni.

[24] A good discussion of medieval parrying can be seen in Grég Mele's paper, "Much Ado About Nothing or the Cutting Edge of Flat Parries," *SPADA*, Union City, 2003.

Chapter 3
Fundamental Concepts

The I.33 system is based on a number of fundamental concepts, which may appear unusual, but which are vital to an understanding of the system. The techniques in I.33 follow a logical progression and all of the fundamental concepts are found in the early pages of the manuscript. However, the concepts are not explicitly described, but they are implicit in the text and illustrations. It is only by performing the actions that are shown and described in the manuscript that the underlying concepts can be understood by a modern interpreter. However well set out I.33 is, the 13th century reader would have had a certain level of basic understanding that the 21st century reader does not have. Neither of the authors, and it is to be hoped none of the readership, has ever witnessed a serious fight with sword and buckler, and as such we come from a position of complete ignorance of the basic flow and structure of the fight. Before moving through I.33 page by page we will introduce the key concepts on which I.33 is based. This will avoid repetition, as these concepts reappear throughout the manual and determine the entire nature of a fight using the I.33 system.

Wards and Counterwards

The first basic concept in I.33 is that of wards and counters. This has a profound effect on the nature and tempo of the fight. At the start of I.33 the anonymous author states that, "It may be observed that in general all combatants, or all men holding a sword in hand, even if they are ignorant of the art of combat, use these seven guards."[1] However, a cursory glance at I.33 reveals what appears to be around twenty guards or ward positions. If there are only seven wards, what are the other positions adopted by the Priest and the Scholar? The author of I.33 describes his first seven positions as *Custodiis* or *wards*, while most of the other positions shown are called *Obsesseo* or *counter*.[2]

The difference between a ward and a counter is that a *ward* is a position which one adopts in preparation to making an attack. A *counter* is a position that one adopts in response to an opponent adopting a ward. Each counter provides a sure defence (as much as any defence can ever be sure) against the obvious attack from the ward that it counters. In many cases the counter also allows an advantageous attack to be made against the warder if the latter does not attack. This leads to some interesting conclusions

First Ward · Underarm

Figure 3.1 *The First Ward, "Underarm." Compare this with the RA MS I.33 illustration on plate 3 (upper), also shown in Chapter 4, p. 93.*

about the tempo of the I.33 fight. Because of the nature of wards and counters it is rarely, if ever, possible to *lie*[3] in a ward as is suggested by many other fencing masters.[4] Rather, once a ward has been adopted, an attack should be made immediately, before the opponent can adopt a counter. If a counter is adopted against a ward, then the warder should immediately attack (though not with the obvious attack that the counter is designed against) or should retreat and adopt another ward or a counter to the counter. I.33's method is built around seizing the opportunities that arise to attack when you are in a favourable position. The manuscript is German after all, and seizing the initiative in a fight was a hallmark of the later Liechtenauer tradition that dominated German fencing in the 14th-16th centuries.[5]

The first example of ward and counter given in I.33 is with the first ward, *Underarm* and its first counter, *Half Shield*. Underarm is held with the sword under the left arm, point backwards and the buckler by the hand, facing either to the left or right. An interesting feature of the artwork in I.33 is that whenever a figure is shown in Underarm his buckler faces out from the page.[6] It is uncertain whether this is deliberate or an artistic artifact, but the authors favour the latter interpretation and adopt Underarm with the buckler facing to the left. Underarm is illustrated at Figure 3.1. Half Shield is the most versatile counter, being used against most of the seven wards. It is illustrated at Figure 3.2.

THE HALF SHIELD COUNTER

Figure 3.2 *The First and most common counter, "Half Shield," often adopted to counter the First Ward.*

This ward and counter are not adopted simultaneously, or by mutual consent. The figures in 3.3 show how two fencers could adopt Underarm and Half Shield. In fig. 3.3 the fight commences out of distance, that is at a distance where neither fencer can hit the other with one foot movement. As the Priest closes to wide distance (that distance at which one fencer can hit the other with one foot movement), he adopts the ward of Underarm. In response the Scholar instantly adopts the counter of Half Shield. As he does this, the Scholar closes range further, but does not come into close distance (the distance at which a blow may be struck without any foot movement).

*Figure 3.3 The adoption of a ward and counter as distance is closed. **A**- Priest and Scholar are out of distance. **B**- the Priest closes to wide distance, adopting Underarm.*

Figures 3.4
Continued from the previous page. A- the Scholar closes distance, adopting Half Shield. B- the Scholar extends his sword to demonstrate that the distance between himself and the Priest is still wide.

So what can be done from this combination of ward and counter? We spoke above of how each counter defeats the obvious attack from the ward it is countering. The obvious attack from Underarm is to the right leg or lower torso of the opponent. These targets seem to be invitingly open, and in fact this is exactly what Half Shield is, an invitation. The text states that "to attack the lower part will be dangerous to his head."[7] If the Priest attacks, the Scholar simply slips his right leg back, cutting him on the head or thrusting him in the face (see below).

Figures 3.5
A-The Priest is in Underarm, the Scholar in Half Shield.
B-The Scholar slips back and strikes the Priest's head.

We also stated above that the counterer usually has an effective attack he can make against a warder who does not attack. In the example of Underarm versus Half Shield the attack is very simple. The Scholar steps forward, cutting at the side of the Priest's head (see figure 3.6).

Now, those people familiar with sword and buckler play as it is usually done by modern re-enactors and stage combatants will probably have looked at Figure 3.5 and asked themselves why the Priest did not guard his head with the buckler as he attacked? Indeed, some later sources recommend precisely this.[8] The answer to this quite logical question lies in the second basic principle of I.33, that of attacking and defending the arm.

Figures 3.6
A- If the Priest remains stationary, the
B-Scholar will bind his arm
and strike him on the head.

ATTACKING AND DEFENDING THE ARM

Let us begin by looking at what might have happened had the Priest made the attack in Figure 3.5, covering his head with his buckler. The Scholar will slip back his right leg as before and instead of cutting at the head, he will cut at the Priest's exposed arm. This is the second basic principle of I.33; it is impossible to cover all potential targets at once with a buckler. The sword arm is the most advanced and exposed target and will be hit if it not defended with the buckler.[9]

Figures 3.7
A- The Priest begins in Underarm.
*B- The Priest attacks the Scholar's legs
while covering his own head.*
*C- The Scholar slips back and strikes the
Priest on the arm.*

Attacking the exposed arm is shown in several places in I.33, and is implied in many more. It is clearly a core principle, one so obvious to the author of the manuscript that he failed to even describe what occurs if the arm is not defended by the attacker.

Whenever an attacker fails to cover the sword arm, the defender should counterattack it. It is not our intention to illustrate an exhaustive list of counter-cuts to the arm from a range of combinations of ward and counter.[10] It is, however, useful to do drills in which an attacker adopts a range of wards and attacks with his arm exposed, giving the defender an opportunity to cut to the arm. Cutting to an exposed arm must become second nature if I.33 is to be successfully used. It is also worth noting that with a steel sword of only a few millimeters thickness, a cut to the arm can be made through a remarkably small gap between sword and buckler. Also note that drills in which the exposed arm is targeted are best done without the attacker having a buckler. If the attacker does the drill while holding a buckler he will be training himself to attack incorrectly, so we feel that it is best done with only the defender having a buckler. Another useful drill is for the defender to target the arm while the attacker tries to cover it with the buckler. This shows up any small openings between the attacker's sword and buckler, and teaches the defender to exploit the slightest gap.

The arm of the defender can also be attacked if he separates sword and buckler to block with the buckler while counterattacking with the sword.[11] As the defender moves to cover with the buckler, the attacking sword and shield should avoid the defender's buckler and cut at his sword arm. The key to being able to do this is to allow your buckler to move naturally, and allow it to draw your sword to the counterattacking arm. This sounds peculiar, but is actually quite natural, particularly if, like the authors, you have previous training whereby simply blocking a cut with a buckler has become second nature. As the defender counterattacks, separating his sword and buckler, you should move your own buckler to block the attack, but follow it closely with your sword. Because your arms are together (so as not to expose the arm to counterattack), moving the buckler to block the counterattack will move the sword to attack the arm of the defender. Whenever the sword arm is extended into distance where it might be hit, it must be defended. If it is not, it can be hit. Therefore defence must be done with sword and buckler together. How is this possible? One method is by using the buckler to extend the length of the sword, effectively turning it into a longsword.

Figures 3.8
A- From the position in Figure 3.7a, the Priest makes an Oberhau which the Scholar defends with his buckler, separating it from his sword.
B- The Priest moves sword and buckler as one to intercept the Scholar's counterattack.

Figures 3.9 *(Continued from previous page) A-Alternatively, as the Priest makes his* Oberhau, *the Scholar parries with his sword, then uncrosses to riposte.* **B-** *In this case the Priest moves his buckler to defend the Scholar's attack and strikes the exposed forearm.*

EXTENDING THE LEGNTH OF THE SWORD--THE STAB-KNOCK[12]

Many systems of combat using long weapons utilize counterattacks made in single time (that is made in the same time as the attack which they counter) where the weapon strikes the opponent while parrying the attack. Such actions are also called *counterattacks with opposition*. Against cuts, counterattacks with opposition are not usually done with shorter weapons, such as the swords shown in I.33, because the weapons simply are not long enough to simultaneously strike and parry.[13] However, these actions are used in I.33. How is this so? Quite simply it is done by using the sword and buckler together to create a dual weapon similar in length and handling characteristics to a longsword.[14] This action is called the Stab-Knock. To deliver a Stab-Knock against an opponent's attack, the sword is used to thrust at the opponent, while the buckler is held alongside the sword-hand and forearm, intercepting the attack. The angle of the thrust is such that, as the counterattack is made, the sword and buckler close the line of the initial attack, parrying the attack simultaneously or fractionally after the counterattack lands.

Like many of the principles in I.33 the Stab-Knock is not described explicitly. It is first mentioned on plate three, where the author of I.33 advises you to "fall under the sword and shield,"[15] and notes "If he is ordinary he will go for your head; you should use a Thruststrike [Stab-Knock]."[16] "Falling under the sword" is an action that is central to I.33, and will be explained in detail below.

Practically any attack into Half Shield (and many attacks into other counters) can be met with a Stab-Knock. The use of Stab-Knocks would appear to be assumed knowledge by the author of I.33, and only a few examples of are explicitly shown. However, a quick look at the possible Stab-Knocks from the most common counter, Half Shield, against direct attacks from the major wards is interesting. It also gives us the opportunity to introduce the other wards.

THE SECOND WARD - RIGHT SHOULDER

We have already looked at the first ward, Underarm, the second ward is called *Right Shoulder*.[17] The obvious attack from Right Shoulder is the *Oberhau Rechts* delivered on a pass forward and right, a formidable and powerful attack. In order to deal with this attack, the defender must parry it before it develops its fullest force, and must also avoid having his weapons swept away by the attacker's buckler. The Scholar should therefore slope step forward and right, while delivering a Stab-Knock in the low line (see figure 3.10) or in the high line.

Figures 3.10
A-The Priest is in Right Shoulder, Scholar counters with Half Shield. B- The Priest passes in with an Oberhau. C- The Scholar slope steps forward and right with a Stab-Knock in the low line.

THE THIRD WARD - LEFT SHOULDER

The third ward is *Left Shoulder*. The obvious attack from here is an *Oberhau Links* diagonally down from left to right. Against this the Scholar can pass forward and left with the left leg, blocking with the buckler and thrusting into the Priest's face.

Figure 3.11a *The Priest is in Left Shoulder, the Scholar counters with Half Shield.*

Figure 3.11b *The Priest passes with an* Oberhau.

Figure 3.11c *The Scholar passes left with a Stab-Knock in the high line.*

Figure 3.11: *The Scholar hides his buckler to show the orientation of the sword hand in* Fourth.

THE FOURTH WARD - VOM TAG

We have termed the fourth ward *vom Tag*. The obvious attack from *vom Tag* is a *Scheitelhau*, a cut directly down onto the head (although a wide range of cuts can be made from this ward).

Against this the Scholar can make the previous defence, or step in and to the right, deflecting the attack with the buckler and thrusting to the face.

Figures 3.12
A- The Priest in vom Tag, *the Scholar counters with Half Shield.* **B-** *The Priest passes in with* Sheitelhau.
C- *The Scholar steps right with Stab-Knock in the high line.*

The Fifth Ward · Nebenhut

We call the fifth ward *Nebenhut*. The obvious attack from *Nebenhut* is a horizontal cut to the lower torso. Against this, the Scholar can slope step forward and right and Stab-Knock in the high line.

Figures 3.13
A- The Priest in Nebenhut, *the Scholar countering with Half Shield.*
B- The Priest passes in with Unterhau.
C- The Scholar slope steps right with Stab-Knock in the high line.

THE SIXTH WARD ‧ PFLUG

The sixth ward we call *Pflug*. The obvious attack from *Pflug* is a thrust. Against this the Scholar can step off the line to the right, deflecting the thrust with his buckler and thrusting to the Priest's face.

Figures 3.14
A- The Priest in Pflug, *the Scholar again countering with Half Shield.* **B-** *The Priest passes in with a thrust.* **C-** *The Scholar steps right with a Stab-Knock in the high line.*

THE SEVENTH WARD ‑ LONGPOINT

For completeness the seventh ward, *Langort* (Long-Point) is shown at Figure 3.14, although no attacks are launched from this ward. Note that three variants of Long-Point are shown in I.33, one where the point is extended downwards at approximately forty-five degrees, a second with the point extended horizontally at chest height, and a third variant where the point is extended up at approximately thirty degrees. We will term these three Low, Middle and High Long-Point respectively.

Figure 3.14 *Low Longpoint.*

Figure 3.15 *Middle Longpoint.*

Figure 3.16 *High Longpoint.*

Unterhau from the First Ward

Lastly, we return to the first ward, Underarm. The obvious attack from Underarm is a horizontal or rising cut (*Unterhau*) on a pass forward and left. Such an attack can be warded in the same way as the attack from Left Shoulder.

This attack, the *Unterhau* from Underarm, is important because it is an attack against which a Stab-Knock cannot be guaranteed successful. The Priest can rapidly change the height of his attack and strike the Scholar under his buckler, which cannot reasonably defend the right-hand side all the way to the ground. Therefore it should be no surprise that the first and most widely illustrated ward in I.33 is Underarm. The primary offensive action in I.33, falling under the sword relies for its success on the flexibility of action possible in an *Unterhau* from Underarm and on the inherent difficulty of defending an attack to the right side unless you are sure what height the attack is being made at.

Figures 3.18 A- *The Priest in Underarm, the Scholar countering with Half Shield.* **B-** *The Priest now passes in with* Unterhau. **C-** *In response the Scholar slope-paces left with Stab-Knock to the Priest's face (with both hands in Fourth).*

FALLING UNDER THE SWORD

Falling under the sword is an action where the attacker binds his opponent's sword from below. When the attacker is in Underarm and is countered by Half Shield, I.33 is explicit about what should and should not be done. The author states:

> "Observe that the First Guard or Under-Arm is represented here, with the opposition being Half Shield. And I advise with good counsel that he who stands in Under-Arm does not deliver any blow, something that can be demonstrated from the "Fool's Guard", because he cannot reach his opponent's upper part, and to attack the lower part will be dangerous to his head; but the one who adopts the opposition can enter and attack him at any time, if he is not kept in check as is written below."[18]

Albersleiben, the "Fools Guard" almost certainly means the German longsword guard of *Alber* in which the sword is held low and in front of the swordsman, with the point directed toward the ground. This makes sense because any cut from here must be a rising cut or an *Unterhau*. The attacker cannot strike the upper body of his opponent with an *Unterhau* because it is covered by the counterer's sword (and can be defended by the Stab-Knock), and he cannot strike the lower body because the counterer will slip back and cut at his head (as illustrated below).

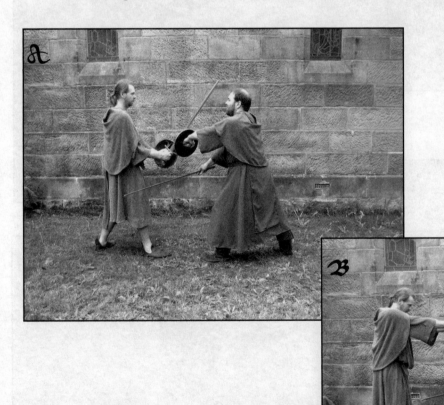

Figures 3.19
A- From the position in 3.18a, the Priest attacks the Scholar's legs. B- The Scholar slips back and strikes the Priest on the head.

ATTACKS AGAINST HALF-SHIELD

Attacks to the lower legs are thus not recommended, while we saw above how the Stab-Knock can defend Half Shield against direct attacks to the body. How then can you attack someone in Half Shield? The author of I.33 writes that from the position shown in RA MS I.33 Plate 3 (upper) with the Priest in Underarm and the Scholar in Half Shield, the Priest must "contain" the Scholar, "as is written below" that is "When Half Shield is adopted, fall under the sword and shield."[19] What this entails is the Priest making a step forward and left (ideally more left than forward) and moving his sword forward into the position shown below.

Figures 3.20 A- *The Priest in Underarm, the Scholar countering in Half Shield.* **B-** *The Priest falls under the sword. In the lower plates, the same maneuver is shown from a different angle.*

The Priest is careful not to bring his body near enough to be hit, but closes enough distance to be able to "contain" the Scholar by closing the Scholar's potential line of attack. From this position a number of actions follow, dictated largely by the reaction of the Scholar. All of these actions are made by the Priest on a pass forward with the left leg. One of these is a Stab-Knock. The author states that "If he is ordinary he will go for your head; you should use a Thruststrike [Stab-Knock]."[20] As the Priest falls

under the sword, the Scholar will attempt to cut downwards onto his head. It is worth noting that if the Priest fails to take his initial step to the left, simply passing forward and left, perhaps in an attempt to make his attack more quickly, he will bring his body into range to be struck before he can close the line of attack with his sword. Without the initial step to take the Priest off the line and allow him to close the Scholar's line, the Scholar's attack is likely to succeed.

Figures 3.21
A- The Priest again assumes Underarm, while the Scholar makes the counter in Half Shield. B- The Priest falls under his sword, omitting his initial slope step left and is struck on the head.

Using the correct footwork, the Priest falls under the sword and the Scholar attempts to cut downward onto his head. The Priest passes forward and left, rolling his buckler over his sword hand so that it faces the right. The buckler deflects the attack while the Priest's point strikes the Scholar in the face. If the buckler had not been present, the sword alone would not have been long enough to perform this action and the Priest would have been struck on the hand or forearm. The same action may be used if the Scholar does not react to the Priest's action (feeling himself covered against any possible attack to the upper body), though in this case the Priest will more likely cut to the right side of the Scholar's head.

Figures 3.22
A- From the start in 3.21a, the Priest falls under the sword.
B- The Scholar strikes at the Priest's head.
C- With a slope pace forward and left, the Priest Stab-Knocks.

Other counter-reactions are [possible]. In Half Shield to provide room to the right to parry the opponent in an attempt a Half-Knock. As [noted] in Figure 3.1c, the attacker [aims] differently to these than he does to the head, if the Scholar is more to the right in an attempt to parry the [attack] the Priest should wait until has to make contact with the Scholar should cut under the Scholar.

Figures 3.23 *An alternate solution.* **A-** *The Priest again begins in Underarm while the Scholar counters in Half Shield.* **B-** *The Priest falls under the sword* **C-** *The Scholar does not react, so the Priest executes a Stab-Knock.*

Other common reactions are for the defender in Half Shield to move his sword across to the right to parry the apparent cut to his head, or to attempt a Stab-Knock in return, as shown in Figure 3.18. The attacker responds quite differently to these than he does to the cut to the head. If the Scholar moves his sword to the right in an attempt to parry the Priest's blade, the Priest should wait until his blade is about to make contact with the Scholar's and then he should cut under the Scholar's hand into his

flank or thigh. The Priest should use the natural motion of his body to assist him in doing this. As he passes forward, his body will rise slightly, matching the upward motion of the blade. As the Priest prepares to land his cut his body will sink. This allows much of the motion of the attack to be made with the body, reducing the motion of the hand and hence disguising the attack from the Scholar.[21] The Priest should react in an almost identical way if the Scholar Stab-Knocks.

Figures 3.25 *A- Starting once again in Underarm, the Priest begins by falling under the sword. **B-** The Scholar attempts to parry. **C-** The Priest cuts under the Scholar's hilt. The sequence is repeated again in 3.26 on the next page, but from a different angle.*

Figures 3.26 *Sequence 3.25 from a different angle.*

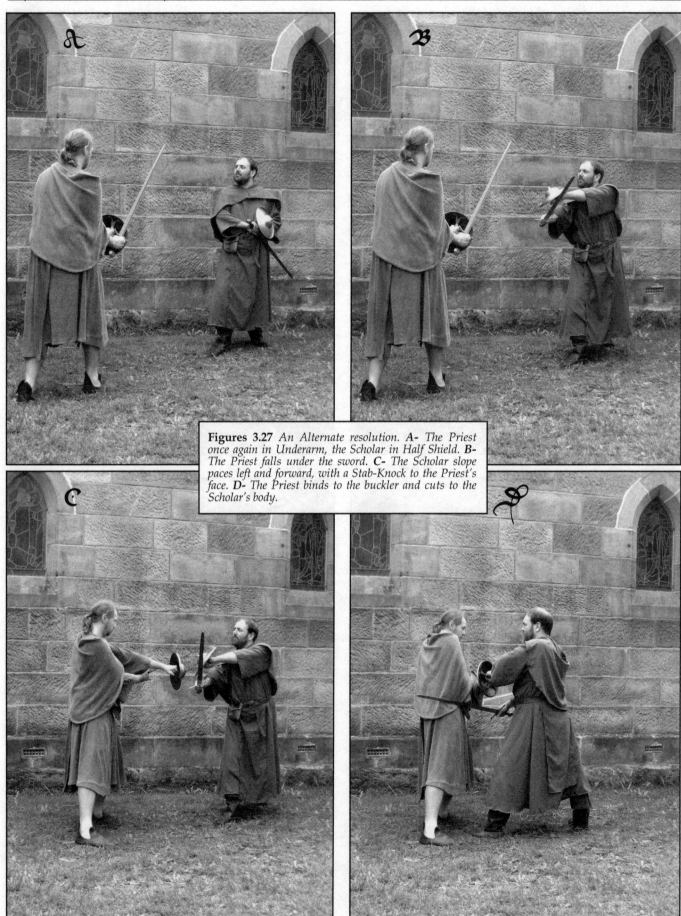

Figures 3.27 *An Alternate resolution.* **A-** *The Priest once again in Underarm, the Scholar in Half Shield.* **B-** *The Priest falls under the sword.* **C-** *The Scholar slope paces left and forward, with a Stab-Knock to the Priest's face.* **D-** *The Priest binds to the buckler and cuts to the Scholar's body.*

BINDING WITH THE SWORD

We have examined what might happen if the Scholar reacts in several natural and instinctive ways to the Priest falling under the sword. If the Scholar cuts to the head or does nothing, the Priest uses a Stab-Knock. If the Scholar parries to his right or Stab-Knocks, the Priest cuts under his guard into his right side or thigh. However, I.33 recommends that the Scholar's correct response is to "counterbind and step."[22] Binding with the sword is another one of the fundamental concepts in I.33.

A bind with the sword is an action where one's sword is pressed against the opponent's sword in order to control and redirect it. According to the author of I.33 the correct response to the Priest falling under the sword is for the Scholar to bind the Priest's sword down to the right with his own, while simultaneously advancing and then using a "Shield-Knock." A Shield-Knock is a bind with the buckler and is the last of the fundamental concepts that will be discussed in this chapter. Therefore the correct response to an opponent who falls under the sword involves two key elements of I.33, binding with the sword and binding with the buckler. To avoid the confusion of introducing two important concepts at once, we will treat binding of the sword in isolation before returning to the Scholar, as he responds to the Priest falling under his sword by binding with the sword and then performing a bind with the buckler, or Shield-Knock.

When the author describes the seven wards he states that "the entire heart of the art of combat lies in this final guard, which is called Long-Point; and all actions of the guards or of the sword finish or have their conclusion in this one, and not in others."[23] The author is not stating here that Long-Point is better than the other wards. To the contrary, he later writes, "Here the first guard or Under-Arm is resumed. The opposition to it will be Long-Point; and it is common and not especially advantageous."[24] What the author is stating is that all actions end

with the arm and point extended, effectively in Long-Point. Therefore since every fencer will repeatedly adopt Long-Point, even if only momentarily, it is important to know what to do from and against it.

Relating this back to falling under the sword, and binding, look at Figure 3.20. The Priest's arm and blade are extended. He is in a variant of Longpoint. The standard response in I.33 to an extended blade is to bind that blade with the sword.

There are four ways in which one blade may bind another blade. In an *overbind*, the binding blade is above the blade being bound. In an *underbind*, the binding blade is below the blade being bound. In either an overbind or an underbind the blade may be bound on the right or left.[25] The bind which the Scholar is advised to do from Half Shield against the Priest falling under the sword is an overbind on the right. This is the most effective of the four binds, because the sword arm is not crossed over the body and, as an overbind, it is assisted by gravity. Therefore the overbind on the right is the bind most often shown in I.33. Moreover, the initial falling under the sword is in itself a kind of bind; an underbind on the right. This is why it is called falling *under* the sword; (the action is under the Scholar's blade, not under his hilt). When the Priest falls under the sword, the author says that he contains the sword of the Scholar. The Priest may bind the Scholar's blade, pressing his blade up and to the right into the Scholar's sword. This controls the Scholar's blade, and allows him to perform the Stab-Knock shown in Figure 3.22.[26] Note also that the overbind which the Scholar is advised to do from Half Shield against the Priest falling under the sword is called a counterbind.[27] Hence falling under the sword must be a bind.

When the Priest falls under the sword, the Scholar is now underbound. He should respond by overbinding the Priest, i.e. by pressing down and to the right with his sword. This is an overbind on the right. As he does this he should enter, that is he should pass forward and right with his left leg. The Scholar can enter because he is in control of the Priest's blade and has taken it off line to the right, where it is harmless, at least for the few moments required by the Scholar to complete his action.

The Scholar has controlled the Priest's sword with his own and now wishes to strike the Priest. As he passes into close distance his concern is preventing the Priest from either renewing his attack with his sword, or parrying the forthcoming cut with his buckler. Fortunately, both these concerns can be addressed by using the last of the fundamental concepts to be discussed in this chapter, binding with the buckler.

Figures 3.28
A- The Priest in Underarm, and the Scholar in Half Shield.
B- As the Priest falls under the sword, the Scholar overbinds to the right.

BINDING WITH THE SHIELD · THE SHIELD-KNOCK

While overbinding and passing forward the Scholar uses his buckler to bind and immobilize the Priest's sword and buckler. This is called a Shield-Knock. As his body moves forward, the Scholar extends his buckler, forcefully striking the Priest's buckler and pressing it into his body. Ideally this will trap the Priest's sword arm under his buckler arm, rendering him almost helpless. The Scholar may then cut at the Priest's face. Throughout I.33, whenever an overbind to the right is made, it is invariably followed by a Shield-Knock. It is perhaps the signature technique of the system.

Figure 3.29a *From the position in 3.28 (top), the Priest falls under the sword.*

Figure 3.29b *To counter, the Scholar binds and advances...*

Figure 3.29c *...Shield-Knocks...*

Figure 3.29d *...and strikes.*

Figures 3.30
A full speed shield knock, filmed with a continuous motor drive. This shows specific timing of each movement for this very important technique.

Timing is critical to the success of a Shield-Knock. The bind with the sword must precede the advance with the body and the actual Shield-Knock, but the movements should flow together as one smooth action. At full speed the bind and the Shield-Knock almost appear simultaneous.

While Figure 3.29 breaks the Shield-Knock down into all of its component actions, Figure 3.31 is an attempt to capture more of the relative timing. The Shield-Knock will be examined more closely in the next chapter.

Figure 3.31a *From the position in 3.30, the Priest falls under the sword and the Scholar binds and advances.*

Figure 3.31b *The Scholar binds with the sword and Shield-Knocks...*

Figure 3.31c *...withdraws his sword...*

Figure 3.31d *...and strikes the Priest.*

The fundamental principles, ward and counter, attacking and defending the arm, extending the length of the sword; the Stab-Knock, binding with the sword and binding with the buckler; the Shield-Knock are all contained in the first four pages of the I.33 manuscript. If all we had were these four pages, we would still have the core of the system. The principles introduced by the author of I.33 in his first four pages recur throughout the remaining sixty. Therefore it is highly recommended that the techniques shown in this chapter be practiced and be thoroughly understood before progressing to the actions described in the remainder of the text.

✄ NOTES ✄

[1] Jeffrey L. Forgeng, *The Art of Medieval Swordsmanship: A Facsimile and Translation of Europe's Oldest Personal Combat Treatise, Royal Armouries MS. I.33*, Union City 2003, Plate 1.

[2] Ibid. (Custodiis– P.1, Obsesseo – P.3).

[3] To lie in a ward means to remain in that ward for a significant space of time.

[4] For example George Silver, *Bref Instruction Upon my Pradoxes of Defence*, (Sloane MS. 376 British Library, C.1605), "Yf yor enemye lye aloft, eyther in open or true gardant fight..." p. 9R.

[5] Christian Tobler *Secrets of German Medieval Swordsmanship* (San Francisco, 2002), "The basic philosophy of Master Liechtenauer's system is summarized in three words: *Maintain the Initiative!*" p. xi.

[6] So for example in plate 22U the buckler faces to the right, while in plate 22L, it faces to the left, despite the fact that the Priest is not supposed to have moved between these two plates.

[7] Forgeng, 2003, Plate 3.

[8] "At Sword and Buckler, keep your left hand extended with your Buckler...and if you cut at his leg, take care to cover your head with your Buckler" Donald MacBane, *The Expert Swordsman's Companion*, 1728, in Mark Rector (ed.), *Highland Swordsmanship*, Union City 2001, p.74.

[9] The importance of protecting the forearm was eloquently explained by John Godfrey in *A Treatise Upon the Useful Science of Defence* (London:1747), p.27; "The most dangerous Cut in the Sword to your Opposer (and which generally carries the keenest Edge) is the Inside Blow at the Wrist...certainly the Cut answers your Ends more than any other, because your Enemy is disabled at once. Any other Cut he may bear for a while, and have a Chance of hitting you, if he continues to fight a little longer; but the Instant you hit him in the Inside of the Wrist, your Victory is secure."

[10] There are many other important reasons for keeping the sword and buckler close together, such as extending the sword and bracing the buckler with the sword during Stab-Knocks, and having the buckler near the sword for binding during Shield-Knocks, both of which are discussed below.

[11] Of course, to do this you must attack in such a way as to force the opponent to make a double-time defence. If you simply attack directly into his shield, for example, you give the opponent a chance to perform a single-time defence, allowing you no time to redirect your sword.

[12] Dr Jeffrey L. Forgeng's preliminary translation of I.33, which the authors have been working from for a number of years, translated the term *stichslac* as "Stab-Knock," rather than "thruststrike" as it appears in later versions of the translation. The authors prefer the former, partly because we are familiar with it, and partly because we think it is more pleasing to the ear and hence easier for fencing students to remember.

[13] For a detailed discussion of counterattacks with opposition, including the effect of weapon length, see: Stephen Hand, *Counterattacks with opposition: The influence of weapon form* in Stephen Hand (ed.) *SPADA* Vol. 1, Union City, 2003.

[14] The German *Langes Schwert* was a weapon approximately 40-50 inches (102-127cm) in total length, with a seven to nine inch (18-23cm) grip and weighing between three and five pounds (1.35-2.25kg). It was designed for use in one hand on horseback or accompanied with a shield, and two hands when used alone on foot.

[15] Forgeng, 2003, Plate 3.

[16] Ibid.

[17] I.33 does not explicitly name all the wards. It states
"The seven guards should begin with Under-Arm;
The second is given to the right shoulder, the third to the left;
Give the fourth to the head, give the fifth to the right side;
Give the sixth to the breast; finally you should have Long-Point." Ibid. Plate 1.
The authors have used the names in the verse where they appear logical and have used other terms where the ward is commonly used and referred to by another historical name within the historical fencing community.

[18] Forgeng, 2003, Plate 3.

[19] Ibid.

[20] Ibid.

[21] Thanks to Colin McKinstry for this insight.

[22] Forgeng, 2003, Plate 3.

[23] Ibid. Plate 2.

[24] Ibid. Plate 31.

[25] The terminology of binding in I.33 may be confusing at first but is incredibly logical. It is usually easy to tell whether a bind is an overbind or an underbind. If there is any doubt, simply bring the swords horizontal. One will be over the other and hence is overbinding the other. Left and right binds can be more confusing, particularly left and right underbinds. This is because all binds are circular and circular movement does not neatly fit into a terminology of over/under and left/right. As you start a bind you can be moving the sword one way, only to move it a very different way further into the bind. Assuming right handed swordsmen a bind to the right is against the right side of the opposing blade, i.e. the outside. Binds on the right move clockwise. A bind on the left is against the left or inside of the opposing blade, and will move counterclockwise.

[26] Interestingly the term "fall under" is used in exactly the same way by the English swordsman George Silver when discussing the sword and buckler fight. Silver states "And if their weapons were short, as in times past they were, yet they could not thrust safe at body or face, because in gardant fight they fall over, or under the perfect crosse of the sword." Silver is saying that if one thrusts at the body of an opponent in his gardant fight (a hanging ward) the opponent will parry down and to his right making a true cross (a parry) with the one's blade bound under his. (Footnote to Paradox 10, George Silver, *Paradoxes of Defence* (1599), in Paul Wagner, *Master of Defence: The Works of George Silver* (2003)).

[27] Forgeng, 2003, Plate 3.

CHAPTER 4
THE FIRST WARD "UNDERARM"

Underarm is the single most widely used ward in I.33. As seen in the previous chapter, all of the fundamental concepts of the system are contained in the first few encounters between Underarm and its counter, Half Shield. We will now look more closely at the specific techniques used from Underarm, and the methods of countering it. Some of this material has already been outlined in the previous chapter, but there is no harm in repeating the basics as often as possible. In fact, the manuscript itself punctuates the sections on each of the other wards by repeating the core sequences from Underarm and Half Shield, and the Priest says "know that all of these are reduced to the first ward and to the counter which is called Half Shield."[1] In addition, it is worth noting that many sequences from other wards, particularly the over- and under-binding techniques used on the various forms of Longpoint, can be directly (and more usefully) applied to the positions adopted from Underarm and Half Shield.

Underarm is held right foot forward, with the sword swept back under the left arm, pointing backwards, right hand by the left hip. In this position the sword is hidden from the opponent, making it difficult for him to judge its length. It may also be noted that it is essentially the same position the sword would sit in its scabbard, perhaps making it difficult for your opponent to even judge whether your weapon has been drawn or not. The functional strengths of the ward, however, are sufficient to recommend it regardless of such considerations.

The buckler is depicted in several different positions, including extended face-on at the opponent, edge-on facing to the right, and edge-on facing to the left, near the sword hand. We favor this last position, as it is important to be able to present the sword quickly, and unless the buckler is held in a withdrawn position, it may foul your own blade.

Why Underarm?
Underarm is the most widely used ward in I.33 for a number of reasons. It is a strong defensive ward, providing a number of simple and effective defences against direct attacks. It may also be used to perform most of the defences described for the major counterwards, such as Half Shield and the Crutch, and thus defend against more sophisticated attacks from most

of the other wards, including Underarm itself. Underarm is also the most favoured ward because it is the most effective position from which to fall under the sword,[2] avoiding the threat of the Stab-Knock. If you are not sure how to respond to the opponent's ward, Underarm is a good choice, as it has both good offensive and defensive potential.

Underarm, and variations upon it, is a commonly depicted stance in later medieval and Renaissance fencing treatises, and its use is well documented.[3] Let us look at Underarm against a variety of direct attacks. It is worth noting here that all these defences are performed primarily with the sword, not the buckler, using the same basic principle as seen with the Shield-Knock.

There are two basic types of defensive footwork used from Underarm against direct attacks by the ordinary fencer, both of which can be illustrated against an attack from the second ward, Right Shoulder. The obvious attack from Right Shoulder is a right *Oberhau*, made at the opponent's head or left shoulder.

If the Priest is in Underarm facing such an attack, he has two possible defences. The first is to use the same movement we have already seen with falling under the sword when the opponent is "ordinary" and "will go for your head."[4] As the Scholar passes forward to attack, the Priest's first step should be to the left with the right foot while raising the sword to underbind the incoming attack. The Priest should then pass forward and left with his left foot, using sword and buckler to deflect the incoming blow away to the right. The buckler can now be used to hold the Scholar in position while he is dispatched. This is also effective against the obvious attacks from *vom Tag*.

Figure 4.1 *The beginning of the play; the Priest in Underarm, the Scholar in Right Shoulder.*

Figures 4.2
A- From the position in 4.1, the Scholar delivers an Oberhau on a pass forward and right.
B- To prevent this, the Priest falls under the sword,
C- deflecting the Scholar's attack with his sword and striking with his buckler, while preparing to deliver a cut of his own...
D- ...or a thrust.

The second option is for the Priest to simply pass forward and left with his left foot, lifting the hilt of his sword to an appropriate height. By aggressively passing forward directly into the origin of the blow, the Priest achieves a strong bind (in this case an Underbind to the right), *Störck* to *Störck*, before the Scholar's blow has built up any force. The Scholar's blade is bound and of no use for the fraction of a second which the Priest needs to uncross his sword and deliver a powerful attack to the Scholar's head. The Priest's only concern is to prevent the Scholar from parrying the forthcoming cut with his buckler. The Priest can use his own buckler to bind the Scholar's, preventing him from parrying. Depending on the position of the Priest's buckler, this might be achieved simply by punching the bucker into the Scholar's shield (using the edge of the buckler to maximize the impact), or by sweeping the Scholar's buckler (and probably his sword as well) away to the left. This defence is also effective against a horizontal or rising cut from *Nebenhut*.

Figures 4.3
A- From the position in 4.1, the Scholar again delivers an Oberhau on a pass forward and right. The Priest passes forward and left, lifting his hilt to bind against the Scholar's sword. Note that the Priest has passed his buckler under his sword arm to protect his elbow against a potential shield-strike by the Scholar.
B- The Priest binds buckler to buckler and strikes the Scholar's head.

Against attacks to the right side of the body, such as a left *Oberhau* from Left Shoulder or a thrust from Pflug, a slight variation is used. The Priest will again pass forward and left with his left foot, lifting the hilt of his sword to an appropriate height, and bring it across his body to the right to cross the incoming attack. The Priest can then use his buckler to hold the Scholar's sword in place while he uncrosses and thrusts his point into the Scholar's belly.

Figures 4.4a *The Scholar in Left Shoulder, the Priest in Underarm.*

Figures 4.4b *The Scholar delivers an* Oberhau *with a pass forward and left.*

Figures 4.4c *The Priest passes forward and left, lifting his hilt to bind against the Scholar's sword.*

Figures 4.4d *The Priest binds with his buckler and thrusts into the Scholar's belly.*

The First counter · Half Shield

The concepts associated with Underarm, Half Shield and falling under the sword are absolutely central to the I.33 system, and although we have already been introduced to the initial techniques in the previous chapter, it is worth going back over them briefly so that their place in the overall flow of the fight becomes clear.

Half Shield is the first counter to Underarm, as well as being a counter to many other wards. It is held right foot forward, with the sword held in front of the body, point up. The point must be elevated by at least forty-five degrees, if not more, as you need to be able to overbind an incoming attack using a downwards swing of the sword. The buckler is held to the left of the blade, covering the swordhand. In the previous chapter we have seen how you can make a counter-attacking Stab-Knock from Half Shield against any simple, direct attack.

In some cases Half Shield is adopted to counter Underarm, in other cases Underarm is adopted to counter Half Shield.[5] In either case, as you form the counter, you should immediately close the distance and attack. This relationship between ward and counter determines the tempo of the fight; you should never lie in a ward while in distance for more than an instant, or your counterer may strike.

Half Shield is a counter to Underarm, not merely a defensive position, because it can directly attack.[6] As seen in Figure 3.6 in the previous chapter, if the Priest in Underarm pauses as the Scholar counters with Half Shield, the Scholar can pass forward, trap the Priest's arm against his own body, and strike his head.

However, the author of I.33 states repeatedly that "when Half Shield is adopted, fall under the sword and shield."[7] The Priest in Underarm ought therefore to attack the Scholar in the instant that he adopts Half Shield, so we will now look at the fight from the point of view

Figure 4.5 *The counter Half Shield. On the mss. plate above, the original manuscript is damaged; hence the incomplete figure.*

ATTACKING FROM UNDERARM: FALLING UNDER THE SWORD

of the Priest as he attacks from Underarm. As soon as the Scholar adopts Half Shield the Priest should immediately fall under the sword by stepping forward and left with the right foot and extending his sword to underbind the Scholar's sword (see figure 3.20 in the previous chapter). As stated in the previous chapter the extension must be aimed high, as if it is intended as a cut to the side of the Scholar's head. This is in order to create a threat and to draw the Scholar's response.

As the first foot movement is completed, there should be a momentary pause. Although momentary, this pause is vital, because it is at this moment that the Priest decides how to continue his attack, depending upon how the Scholar has reacted. The ordinary fencer might respond with one of several reactions, which are detailed in the previous chapter. Firstly, the Scholar may not react, in which case he should be struck in the face with a thrust or on the right side of the head with a blow. The same action may be used if the Scholar tries to attack the head of the Priest (Fig. 3.22). The Scholar may

parry to the right with his sword, in which case the Priest should undercut his parry, striking him in the flank or leg (Fig. 3.26) or the Scholar may attempt to Stab-Knock, in which case the Priest should also undercut, hitting the Scholar in a similar fashion (Fig. 3.27)

Two other reactions are possible. Because of the danger of having the Priest's attack undercut his parry, the Scholar may instead attempt a simple point-down parry. As the Priest falls under the sword, the Scholar could simply rotate his sword down to cross the attack, preventing the Priest from cutting under his hilt. This position strongly resembles another of the I.33 counter-wards, the Crutch. The problem with this defence, however, is that the Scholar effectively traps his own sword underneath the Priest's, and cannot withdraw it to riposte; the Scholar has helped underbind himself! The Priest can simply transfer the overbind from his sword to buckler and continue to attack with an offensive Shield-Knock of his own - this is called *Treading Through*, and we will see numerous examples of similar Tread-Throughs throughout the manuscript.

Figure 4.6 *Half Shield employed as a counter against the First Ward, Underarm.*

Figures 4.7 (from the position in fig. 4.6)
A- The Priest falls under the sword, the Scholar adopts the Crutch.
B- The Priest Treads-Through, passing forward and left, binding with the buckler and executing a thrust.

Figure 4.8
Buckler strike from Jörg Wilhalm's fechtbüch of 1520.

The second possible reaction of the Scholar is to separate his sword and buckler, parrying as above with his sword, but using the buckler as a weapon to counterattack. Although no such offensive use of the buckler is illustrated or described in I.33, it is a technique illustrated in other German sources (such as Jörg Wilhalm's *fechtbüch* from c.1520), and would seem to be a natural and instinctive reaction, so it is worth addressing.

The defence shown in figures 4.9a-c below requires subtle timing, as the Scholar must wait for the Priest to commit to his undercut before dropping his point for the parry; otherwise, the Priest can cut over the Scholar's hilt and strike him in the face or the buckler arm.

As stated above, I.33 does not illustrate such a defence, but the problem with it is fairly obvious and the Priest's response is almost inevitable. As the Scholar parries the Priest's attack, he punches his buckler at the Priest's face. The Priest's instinctive reaction is to flinch back while raising his buckler, and with it his sword. By continuing this motion, he will strike the Scholar's buckler-arm with considerable force.

Figures 4.9a *From the position in 4.6, the Priest falls under the sword.*

Figures 4.9b *The Scholar passes into Crutch and parries.*

Figures 4.9c *The Scholar then strikes the Priest in the face with the buckler.*

Figures 4.9d *Alternatively, the Priest leans back and thrusts at the Scholar's face.*

Figures 4.10
A-The Priest is in Underarm, the Scholar is in Half Shield.
B-The Priest falls under the sword while the Scholar attempts a shield strike,
C- but the Priest leans back and cuts up at the Scholar's buckler-arm.

Defending from Half Shield ⁃ The Shield Knock

None of these instinctive reactions to the Priest's attack are effective, so how should the Scholar react? As we have seen in the previous chapter, the advice of I.33's author is to "counterbind and step"[8] with either a Shield-Knock or a grapple. The key to the Shield-Knock is that it is done immediately and aggressively. If the Scholar allows the Priest to commence his second foot movement, or is too tentative in his execution of the Shield-Knock, the defence will not work. It is a rather brutal but devastatingly effective technique.

The first part of the defence is to bind the Priest's sword down to the right. This is achieved by the Scholar passing directly into the attacking sword and striking the rising *störck* of the Priest's sword with the *störck* of his own with a fairly vigorous downward push. The Scholar must use the edge of his sword to achieve the bind, as he is directly opposing the force of the Priest's rising cut. It is important to note that the Scholar is moving directly at the Priest's sword, not directly into the Priest himself. There can be some variation in how this bind can work; if the Scholar binds the Priest's sword early, before his extension is complete, it works best as a push or punch directly downwards. If the Priest's extension is almost complete, a more vigorous action, more of a beat, made more to the right may be necessary.

The second part of the movement follows immediately, and at full speed appears almost simultaneous. As soon as the Priest's sword is bound, the Scholar should push his buckler strongly into the Priest's buckler. If this is where it should be, on top of the Priest's sword-arm, this should trap both his sword and buckler against his body, giving the Scholar the moment he needs to recover his sword and strike the Priest on the head. Note that if the Priest's buckler is not on top of his sword-arm, then he will have exposed his arm as he falls under the sword. The Scholar should have taken the opportunity to strike the Priest's arm rather than attempting a Shield-Knock.

The three separate elements of the Shield-Knock, (the overbind with the sword, the bind with the buckler and the cut to the head) should flow together as one smooth action, and be completed as quickly and vigorously as possible. It is worth noting here that Plate 61 of I.33 shows the Scholar winding up for the riposte after a Shield-Knock, and has drawn his sword back into something resembling the ward of *vom Tag* (see Chapter 7); the riposte is thus obviously designed to be a powerful cut capable of killing the opponent outright (see figures 4.11 p. 104).

**Figures 4.11
(from the position in 4.10 top)**
A-The Priest falls under the sword.
B-The Scholar binds and advances,
C-and Shield-Knocks.

It is possible that the Priest, having had his sword bound, will separate his buckler from his sword arm and raise it to prevent it being trapped also, or perhaps even attempt to strike the Scholar with it. In this case, the Scholar should ignore the Priest's buckler, and bind his buckler against the Priest's sword arm only. Then all the Scholar need do is bring his point on line and thrust into his opponent's body.[9]

Figures 4.12
(From the position in fig. 4.10 top)
A-The Priest falls under the sword, and the Scholar passes forward to bind. Note that the Priest is separating sword and buckler, B-generously allowing the Scholar to thrust upward into his chest.

The bind with the buckler is vital in preventing the Priest's sword from being brought back into the fight while the Scholar completes his defence. It is noted in I.33 that the "ordinary combatant" will often omit the Shield-Knock.[10] In this instance the Scholar, having bound the Priest's sword, will immediately raise his arm to strike at the Priest's head without pinning the Priest's sword and shield with his buckler. In this case, the Priest will be free to attack with the same rising action used in falling under the sword, striking the Scholar's sword arm in mid-swing.[11]

Figures 4.13
(From the position in 4.10 top)
A-The Priest falls under the sword and the Scholar passes forward to bind. The angle of the photograph makes it appear that the Scholar has performed a Shield-Knock, when in fact his buckler is to the Priest's right.
B-Scholar draws back the sword to strike,
C-and the Priest falls under the sword again and hits the Scholar's arm.

The alternative defence is for the Scholar to grapple the Priest by enveloping his arms.[12] This can be done if the bind has not been successful in pressing down the Priest's sword, or if the Scholar has moved a little late and the Priest's sword is high and his extension is close to complete. After binding the sword, the Scholar can pass his buckler over or under the Priest's arms, wrapping them under his left arm while performing a half incartata with his right foot. This enables the Scholar to capture both of the Priest's weapons, and leaves the Scholar's sword free for a lethal cut or thrust.

Figures 4.14
(From the position in fig. 4.10 top)
A-The Priest falls under the sword and the Scholar binds.
B- This time the Scholar grapples underneath the Priest's arms while making a half incartata.

DEFENDING THE SHIELD-KNOCK

The Shield-Knock is the signature technique of the I.33 system but it is not invincible. So how does the attacker get out of this bind? The author of I.33 offers three suggestions, "Treading Through, exchange of sword, or with the right hand he can seize the sword and shield."[13] All rely upon a deception, and are performed as a response to an attempted Shield-Knock by the defender.

Durchtrit: The Tread-Through

The Tread-Through is in essence an offensive Shield-Knock. There are several ways of doing a Tread-Through, but we will begin with a Tread–Through that works by deceiving the opponent's Shield-Knock.

Let us suppose the Priest falls under the sword, and the Scholar passes forward in an attempt to bind the Priest's blade. The Priest can deceive this defence by quickly withdrawing his sword and sweeping it down and across the front of his body, leaving nothing but empty air for the Scholar's sword to bind against. It does not really matter if the Scholar makes brief contact with the Priest's blade as it withdraws, as this will only help it in its way. Also, if the Scholar's bind is hesitant or ineffective (for example, if he has bound the *schweck* of the Priest's blade rather than the *störck*), the same withdrawal of blade can be achieved even after the bind.

The completion of the technique depends upon the success of the Priest's deception. The Priest should leave his buckler in place, so that the Scholar who has committed himself to a vigorous defence, will bind the Priest's buckler with his own. The Priest should encourage the Scholar to continue pressing by binding back vigorously, trapping the Scholar's buckler against his. The Scholar's buckler is not available to parry the sword, and the Priest can continue his sweep up and around in an anti-clockwise compass, to strike at the left side of the Scholar's head. In effect the Priest has fooled the Scholar into binding his own buckler against the Priest's and thereby removing his own defence.

Note that the Priest could have struck the Scholar's legs instead. However, such a cut might not be completely disabling, and would leave the angry and wounded Scholar with a chance to strike the Priest on the head before he collapsed. There are a number of such instances in I.33 where a combatant passes up a chance for an easy but non-lethal blow, pursuing instead a more difficult but more certainly deadly strike. Such techniques indicate more than anything else the seriousness of I.33's intent.

Figure 4.15a
The Priest in Underarm, the Scholar in Half Shield.

Figure 4.15b
The Priest falls under the sword, and the Scholar binds and advances.

Figure 4.15c
The Priest disengages under the Scholar's bind...

Figure 4.15d
...circles his sword in an anti-clockwise direction...

Figure 4.15e
...continues circling...

Figure 4.15f
...and strikes the Scholar's head.

Mutacio Gladii: **Changing Sword**

Changing Sword is a variation of the above technique, which occurs when the Scholar does not fully commit to the Shield-Knock. Failing to bind against the Priest's sword, the Scholar ought not to continue to press forward with his buckler, as the Shield-Knock should only follow the bind with the sword. In this case, the Scholar's buckler is still free to move, and may well be lifted to intercept the Priest's cut. Therefore, instead of landing the cut, the Priest should continue his anti-clockwise compass a full 360 degrees, back to where it would have been had he completed falling under the sword. The Scholar's buckler should naturally follow the swinging sword, looking for an opportunity to block the blow. If it does not, the Priest should immediately strike to the first available opening.

The practical result of this is that, at the completion of the compass, the Priest's sword will end up on top of the Scholar's; in I.33's language, the Priest will have overbound the Scholar on the left. At the same time the Priest can bring his buckler back into play, binding vigorously against the Scholar's sword and (if possible) buckler, trapping both sword and buckler against the Scholar's body, and striking upwards into his face. Although this may appear complicated, it is in practice a quick and very natural movement

Figures 4.16
A-The Scholar passes forward to bind.
B- The Priest sweeps his sword up and around at the Scholar's head, causing the Scholar to raise his buckler.

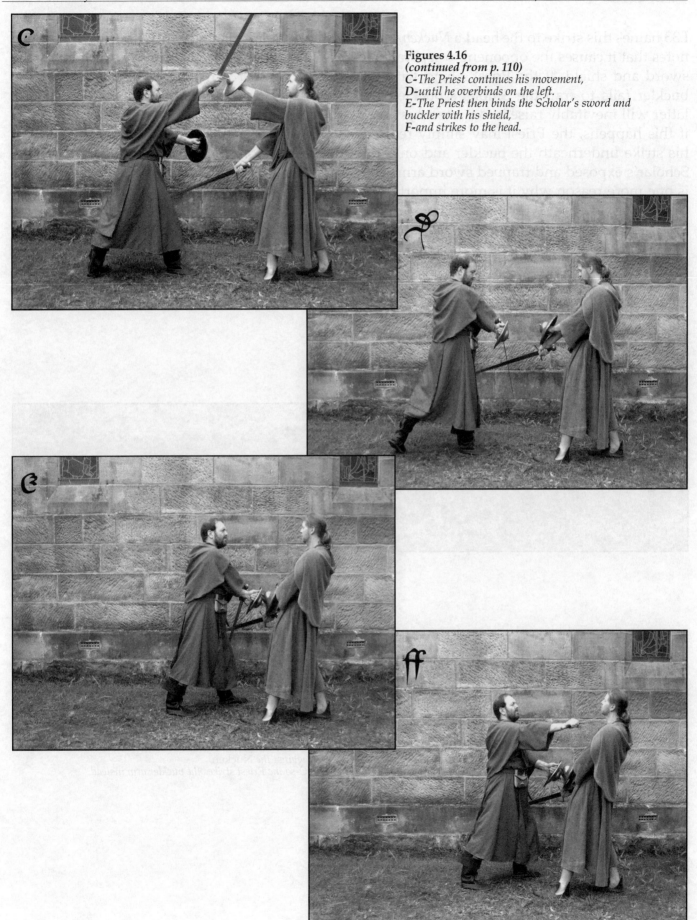

Figures 4.16
(continued from p. 110)
C-*The Priest continues his movement,*
D-*until he overbinds on the left.*
E-*The Priest then binds the Scholar's sword and buckler with his shield,*
F-*and strikes to the head.*

I.33 names this strike to the head a *Nucken*,[14] and notes that it causes the opponent to separate his sword and shield. If the Priest's bind with the buckler fails to trap the Scholar's buckler, the latter will inevitably raise it to protect his head; if this happens, the Priest may simply redirect his strike underneath the buckler and onto the Scholar's exposed and trapped sword arm. This is one more reason why it is more important to trap the opponent's sword than his buckler.

If the Scholar manages to withdraw his sword arm to strike before it can be overbound, the Priest's *nucken* can simply be made into the Scholar's exposed right forearm.

It is also noted in I.33 that the Priest should not delay in his *nucken*, or his sword arm may be grappled.[15] The Scholar can simply pass forward, extending his buckler arm underneath both of the Priest's arms, and envelop them, with his buckler over the top of the Priest's sword.

Figures 4.17
A-The Priest has overbound on the left.
B- The Scholar moves his buckler to cover against the Nucken,
C-so the Priest strikes the buckler arm instead.

Figure 4.18a *The Priest overbinds on the left. From this point both sequences below begin.*

Figure 4.18b *The Scholar withdraws his sword...*

Figure 4.18c *...so the Priest strikes the Scholar's sword arm.*

Figure 4.18d *Alternatively, the Priest pauses; the Scholar takes advantage by passing forward and grappling...*

Figure 4.18e *...the Scholar continues to pass forward, leading with his heel (an incartarta), throwing the Priest off balance...*

Figure 4.18f *...and finishes with a thrust. Note that the Scholar's buckler is above, and the Priest's below.*

Seizing Sword and Shield

The Priest can also use this circular overbind to grapple the Scholar, particularly if either fencer has been a little too enthusiastic in closing the distance. Rather than establishing the overbind and cutting to the head, the Priest performs an incartata to the right with his left foot as his sword reaches the top of its arc, and envelops the Scholar's arms from above with his sword arm.

At this point the Scholar is safely held and contained. The Priest may now use his buckler-hand to disarm the Scholar; if he resists, the Priest may deliver a sharp buckler strike to the face. This will have a powerful calming effect and will make the Scholar more cooperative.

Once the Scholar is disarmed, the Priest may stab him with his own weapon. Alternatively the Priest may simply throw the Scholar to the floor very roughly.[16]

If he acts quickly, the Scholar can escape from this grapple. As soon as his arms are enveloped by the Priest's sword arm, he should let go of both sword and buckler, extract his arms, and either wrestle the Priest or run away. If the Scholar is lucky, his buckler will land on the Priest's foot, distracting him for a moment (be careful with this!). The Priest must, therefore, be wary of the Scholar releasing his weapons, and be ready to bring his sword to bear quickly if the Scholar escapes the grapple.

Figures 4.20
A-From the overbind...
B- ...the Priest sweeps his sword up and around at the Scholar's head. The Scholar follows with his buckler.
(continued in figs. 4.21 p. 115)

Figures 4.21 *(continued from fig. 4.20 p. 114)*
C-Realizing that he is too close to overbind, the Priest grapples over the Scholar's outstretched arms.
D-The Priest now passes forward, leading with the heel (an incartata) and throws his hip into the Scholar's, breaking his balance.
E-The Priest continues to rotate his body,
F-throwing the Scholar to the ground,
G-where he can discuss the situation from a position of strength.

Figures 4.22
A-The Priest grapples the Scholar's arm with his sword arm.
B-The Scholar drops his weapons,
C-and grabs the Priest's shoulders,
D-kicking him soundly in the back.
(The play can end here or be continued as shown on the facing page)

Figures 4.22: (continued from p. 116)
E-The Priest prevents the grapple by bringing his sword to bear in Pflug.
F-The Scholar has no choice but to flee,
G-leaving the Priest to collect the Scholar's weapons at his leisure.

RE-ESTABLISHING THE BIND

All three of these responses to a Shield-Knock— the *Tread-Through, Change of Sword* and *Seizing Sword and Shield*—begin the same way, by moving the sword out of the way of the bind. As shown above, attempting to block the circular bind with the buckler is not, on its own, an effective defence. So what can the Scholar do?

The answer is for the Scholar to reestablish the overbind.[17] If the Scholar passes forward in an attempt to bind the Priest's sword and the latter deceives the bind, then the Scholar needs to do two things. The first is to raise his buckler to protect his head. This will force the Priest

to complete his circular overbind, rather than use the Tread-Through. The second action the Scholar must make is an anti-clockwise compass with his sword, following the Priest's weapon as closely as possible. If the Scholar is adept at keeping sword and buckler together, this movement will flow quite naturally.

At the end of his compass, the Scholar will have overbound the Priest, just as he would have had his initial bind been successful. The Scholar can then complete his Shield-Knock.

Figures 4.24
A-The Priest in Underarm, the Scholar in Half Shield.
B- The Priest falls under the sword while the Scholar passes forward to bind.
(continued page facing)

Figures 4.24:(continued from facing page)

C-The Priest sweeps his sword around anticlockwise.
D-The Scholar circles both sword and buckler around in the same direction, following the Priest,
E-overbinding him on the right,
F-and performing a Shield-Knock.

CONTRARY AND IRATE: FLEEING THE SHIELD-KNOCK

While the previous responses depend upon the Priest deceiving the Scholar's bind, it is always possible that these will fail, and the Scholar will succeed in binding both sword and buckler during the Shield-Knock (either initially or by rebinding as discussed above). What should the Priest do if the Scholar's bind is successful? In several places throughout the manuscript the author has included a little rhyme, designed (presumably) to remind the combatants what to do when bound in a Shield-Knock:

> *The one who binds and the one who is bound*
> *are contrary and irate;*
> *The one who is bound flees to the side;*
> *I seek to pursue*[18]

Elsewhere in I.33 it is noted that "the one who has been bound can flee where he will, either to the left or to the right."[19] Fleeing to the left is the easier and quicker of the two, because the body is already moving in that direction. As the Scholar pushes against the Priest's buckler, all the Priest need do is complete his intended foot movement, passing his left foot around and to the left, perhaps a little more widely than he was initially intending. This will allow the Priest's buckler to slip out from underneath the bind, after which he can raise it to protect his head from the Scholar's sword. The Priest can then pass backward again with the right foot, and thrust his sword at the Scholar's belly. Although the Scholar can deflect this with his buckler fairly easily, it does at least discourage him from following too closely.

Figures 4.25 *The Priest in Underarm, the Scholar in Half Shield. (play continues on page facing).*

Figures 4.25
(continued from facing page)
B-The Priest falls under the sword, the Scholar binds and advances.
C-The Priest starts to move left as the Scholar completes his bind,
D-slope pacing forward and left with his left foot, while bringing his point on-line with the Scholar's belly, and thrusting.

Fleeing to the right is perhaps a little more difficult, but has some advantages, including the fact that is it unexpected, and produces more opportunity for striking a palpable hit. The timing, however, is subtle. Once the Priest has completed the step to the left with his right foot, the Scholar passes forward to bind the sword and pin down the Priest's buckler with his own. As this happens, the Priest should bring his left foot forward and right (relative to its original position) i.e. a half *incartata*. It is also important for the Priest not to resist the Scholar's buckler, as he needs to encourage the Scholar to extend his arm and commit to the Shield-Knock. On completion of the half incartata, the Priest's sword will be freed from the bind and in an ideal position to deliver a false edge cut to the Scholar's extended buckler arm. Having struck the Scholar's arm, the Priest can recover by passing backwards again, delivering a parting thrust to the Scholar's face or belly on the way out.

Note that this rising cut to the arm, despite being performed with the false edge, is a deceptively powerful cut to a very vulnerable target. Extra care must be exercised when performing this technique.

Figures 4.26
A-The Priest in Underarm,
the Scholar in Half Shield.
B- The Priest again falls under his sword while
the Scholar binds and advances.
(play continues page facing)

Figures 4.26
(continued from previous page)
C-The Priest makes a half incartata, *freeing his sword*
from the bind,
D-*then cuts up at the Scholar's arms with his false edge,*
E-*passes back, slicing as he withdraws the blade,*
F-*and thrusting at the Scholar's belly.*

After fleeing to the right, there are a number of reasons why the Priest might not be able to strike the Scholar's arm. The Priest may move too early, the Scholar may not extend his left arm enough while binding the Priest's buckler, or the Priest may move too late, giving the Scholar a chance to recover his sword after the bind. In these cases, there is a variation on the above technique. Although it may appear complicated, in practice it flows very naturally.

The Priest falls under the sword, stepping forward and left with the right foot as before. As the Scholar passes to Shield-Knock, the Priest should bring his left foot forward and right with a half *incartata* in the same way. The Scholar may try to strike the Priest's head, but the sideways movement will have freed the Priest's buckler so that the latter can defend himself. The Priest now uses his sword, not to cut upwards, but to envelop the Scholar's arms by sweeping upwards. The Priest thus traps both the Scholar's sword and buckler in the crook of his right arm.

At this point the Scholar is safely held and contained. All the Priest need do now is to transfer control from his sword arm to his shield arm. The Priest wraps his buckler over the top of the Scholar's arms, keeping a tight grip. When the grapple is safely on, the Priest releases the grip with his sword arm and strikes the Scholar with his sword. As discussed earlier, a struggling Scholar can be pacified with one or more sharp raps to the face with the buckler.

Figures 4.27
A- From the bind,
B- the Priest flees to the right.
C- As the Scholar prepares to strike him,
D- the Priest raises his buckler to block the blow.
E- As the Scholar makes his blow, the Priest raises his sword arm to grapple,
F- binding the Scholar's arms.
G- The Priest then passes forward, wrapping his buckler arm over the Scholar's arms. As he releases his sword arm he slices across the Scholar's belly,
H- and lines up his point for a finishing thrust.

As in the previous example of such a grapple, if the Scholar acts quickly, he can escape from this. As soon as his arms are enveloped by the Priest's sword arm, he should let go of both sword and buckler, extract his arms, and wrestle or flee. The Priest must therefore be wary of the Scholar releasing his weapons, and be ready to bring his sword to bear quickly if the Scholar escapes.

Figures 4.28
A-From the position in figure 4.27f (previous page), the Scholar drops his weapons,
B- and grapples from behind.
C- The Priest prevents this by spinning into Pflug.

Fig. 4.29 *The setup to the grapple on p. 125.*

CUTTING UNDER THE BIND

It may seem that as he falls under the sword, the Priest can cut under the Scholar's overbind. The Priest, seeing the Scholar binding and advancing, may simply allow his sword to arc downwards into the Scholar's legs. In practice, if the Priest attempts this, one of several things happens. Firstly, the Scholar may bind the Priest's blade down so that it misses. Secondly, the Scholar may bind the Priest's sword down into the ground. Lastly, the Priest's sword may be only partially bound and may strike the Scholar in the leg. It is doubtful whether such a cut would inflict enough damage to prevent the Scholar from completing his Shield-Knock and delivering a far more damaging blow to the Priest.[20] Therefore, while cutting under the bind seems like a logical thing to do, experimentation suggests that it was not included for the very good reason that it didn't work.

Figures 4.30
A-Priest in Underarm, Scholar in Half Shield.
B-The Priest falls under the sword, the Scholar binds and advances, the Priest responding with an undercut and misses the Scholar's legs.
C- The Scholar Shield-Knocks (note that as shown in 4.12, he targets the Priest's sword, not his buckler).
D- Alternatively, the Priest falls under the sword, while the Scholar binds and advances. The Priest undercuts, but this time the Scholar binds down and into the ground.
E-The Scholar then Shield-Knocks.
F-Alternatively, the Priest and Scholar begin with the same actions, but the Priest undercuts and strikes the Scholar in the leg.
G- The enraged Scholar ignores the injury and Shield-Knocks anyway.

THE SECOND COUNTER ⁃ THE CRUTCH

The second counter used against Underarm is the Crutch. Unlike Half Shield, which counters several wards, the Crutch is only adopted as a counter to Underarm. The right leg is forward, with the sword held point hanging down with the hilt at chin height[21] and the buckler facing to the left. This can be an uncomfortable position if held for any length of time, and for the most part I.33 shows the sword hanging vertically downwards, indicating a loose grip on the weapon.

The Crutch offers a defence with the sword against any attack the Priest can reasonably make from Underarm. If the Priest attacks into the Scholar's sword his attack will simply be parried and the Scholar will pass forward, grappling the Priest's arms from underneath and thrusting him in the belly or face.

Figure 4.31 *The Crutch.*

Figures 4.32
A-The Priest in Underarm, the Scholar in Crutch.
B-The Priest attacks directly into the Scholar's counter in an attempt to overbind it.
C- The Scholar passes forward, parries and grapples.
D-The Scholar thrusts to the face.

The Crutch would seem to leave the head vulnerable. This is, of course, an illusion. If the Priest is foolish enough to strike to the Scholar's head, the Scholar merely lifts his buckler to block the blow while raising his sword point a little and lunging forward to deliver a Stab-Knock to the Priest's belly.

Figures 4.33
A-The Priest in Underarm, the Scholar in Crutch.
B-This time the Priest passes forward with a Sheitelhau.
C- The Scholar lunges forward with a Stab-Knock.

If the Priest attacks the Scholar's hands, the Scholar may *wind*[22] or rotate his hands clockwise, passing forward and left and Stab-Knocking to the Priest's face.

This is the same response that can be used against the Priest if he fails to respond immediately to the Scholar's counter.

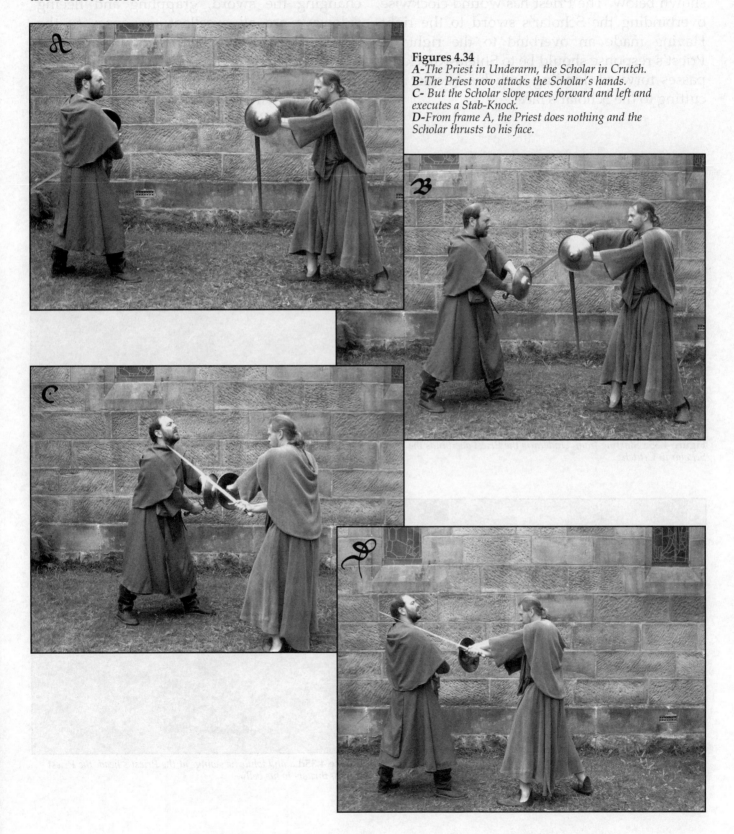

Figures 4.34
A-*The Priest in Underarm, the Scholar in Crutch.*
B-*The Priest now attacks the Scholar's hands.*
C- *But the Scholar slope paces forward and left and executes a Stab-Knock.*
D-*From frame A, the Priest does nothing and the Scholar thrusts to his face.*

In order to avoid this fate, the author of I.33 advises that when the Scholar adopts the Crutch, the Priest should either bind at once or adopt the Crutch himself. The first response is shown below. The Priest has wound clockwise, overbinding the Scholar's sword to the right. Having made an overbind to the right the Priest's response should be to Shield-Knock. He passes forward, binding with his buckler and cutting to the Scholar's face.

According to the author of I.33 once the bind preceding the Shield-Knock commences, "immediately all the things ensue that you had before."[23] This is not strictly true. While changing the sword, grappling and fleeing sideways are all excellent responses to the Priest's Shield-Knock, the Tread Through does not work. This is because the distance is greater than in the example with Underarm and Half Shield and therefore if the Scholar removes his blade as the Priest Shield-Knocks, the Priest's point will be a threat.

Figure 4.35a *Starting from Underarm the Priest overbinds the Scholar in Crutch.*

Figure 4.35b *And finishes with a Shield-Knock.*

Figure 4.35c *From the bind above, this time the Scholar removes his blade...*

Figure 4.35d *...and while he swings at the Priest's head, the Priest simply thrusts to his belly.*

The different ward and distance also means that the Change of Sword works differently, but in this case it is more effective. As the Priest overbinds, the Scholar disengages over the top of the bind, rotating the point anticlockwise and re-engages the Priest's blade on the outside line. The Scholar can now pass forward and Shield-Knock, freeing his blade for a thrust to the belly.

Figures 4.36
A-The Priest in Underarm, the Scholar in Crutch.
B-The Priest opens with an overbind,
C- but the Scholar removes his blade.
D-The Scholar disengages over the bind and re-engages on the outside line.
E- The Scholar finishes with a Shield-Knock.

The grapple done by the Scholar against the Priest as he attempts to Shield-Knock is quite different from those grapples seen previously. As the Priest overbinds, the Scholar should immediately pass forward, moving his buckler down and to the left and then enveloping the arms of the Priest from underneath. The Scholar should not withdraw his sword from the Priest's bind until he has started to wrap his buckler arm around the arms of the Priest. At this point he should draw his sword up and away from the Priest's sword. The Scholar may then draw his sword back for a finishing thrust.

Figures 4.37
A-Priest in Underarm, Scholar in Crutch.
B-The Priest overbinds.
C- The Scholar responds by slope pacing forward and left, passing his buckler arm under the Priest's arms,
D- grappling,
E- and finishing with a thrust.

Because of the orientation of the Scholar's sword, he cannot really flee to his left as the Priest binds and Shield-Knocks. He can, however, flee very effectively to the right. The Scholar steps right with his right foot, followed by his left and cuts up at the Priest's arms with his true edge. The Scholar can then pass back, turning his hand clockwise into third position and thrusting with his sword into the Priest's belly.

Figures 4.38
A- From the overbind,
B- the Scholar steps to the right,
C- and cuts upward at the Priest's arms,
D- before passing back and thrusting.

The second response which the Priest can make to the Scholar's counter of the Crutch is to adopt the Crutch in return. This places the Priest and the Scholar in one of the few symmetrical binds in I.33. The actions which follow can be made equally well by the Priest and the Scholar, but the Priest, being the one who created the bind, has a slight initiative. The Priest rotates counter clockwise into third position and thrusts at the Scholar in opposition.

Figures 4.39
A-Priest engages the Scholar in the Crutch.
B-The Priest turns his hand and thrusts the Scholar in the belly.

In order to prevent this, the Scholar cuts at the right side of the Priest's head as soon as he binds. The Priest winds his sword up and to the right to parry the Scholar's attack, rotating his hand into fourth position as he does so. He then binds down the Scholar's sword, passes forward and Shield-Knocks.

Figures 4.40
A- *From the engagement in 4.39a (facing page), the Scholar this time cuts at the Priest's head.*
B- *Using the false edge, the Priest parries on the outside,*
C- *and overbinds to the right, then Shield-Knocks.*

THE THIRD COUNTER - LONGPOINT

The Third Counter against Underarm is *Longpoint*. The author of I.33 says that "the entire heart of the art of combat lies in this final guard, which is called Long-Point; and all actions of the guards or of the sword finish or have their conclusion in this one, and not in others."[24] As seen in Chapter 3, what this statement means is that at the end of most actions a fencer's sword will be extended in Longpoint, and hence it is important to know what to do from and against it. There are three variants of Longpoint. The one shown as a counter to Underarm is Extended Longpoint

It is clear that, while moving into Longpoint during the course of other actions is inevitable,

the author of I.33 has a very low opinion of Longpoint as a counter. He states that Longpoint is "common and not especially advantageous."[25] No direct attacks are made by the Priest in Underarm against the Scholar in Longpoint. The current authors have experimented with a range of attacks against this counter, none of them successful. Any direct attack against a competent fencer in Longpoint will result in the attacker spitting himself on the defender's point. However, while Longpoint is virtually proof against attacks, it is appallingly vulnerable to the blade being bound. The author of I.33 tells us that "When Longpoint is adopted, at once bind below and above." but "a bind above will always be more useful than one below."[26]

Figure 4.41 *Extended Longpoint.*

The first bind described against Longpoint is the most favoured bind in I.33, the overbind on the right. From Underarm the Priest passes forward, overbinding the Scholar's blade to the right. From there the Priest completes a Shield-Knock.

Figures 4.42
*A-The Priest in Underarm, the Scholar counters
with Longpoint.
B- The Priest overbinds,
C- and Shield-Knocks,
D- cutting to the Scholar's face.*

The other bind that can be easily made by the Priest from Underarm is an underbind on the right. The Scholar responds by overbinding the Priest on the right. The Priest may be intentionally making an underbind or he may be attempting the overbind above and being thwarted by the Scholar making his own overbind as the Priest raises his sword. In all cases the Priest's response will be identical, regardless of how he got there.

Obviously from the overbind, the Scholar will seek to Shield-Knock. In response to this, the Priest will change sword. Because the initial bind is occurring at a very wide distance and with the blades at a low angle to each other, changing sword is by far the preferable response, involving a very subtle disengage over the Scholar's sword and a re-binding in the outside line. Once the change of sword is complete, the Priest may Shield-Knock and *nucken*.

Figures 4.43
A-Priest in Underarm, Scholar in Longpoint.
B-The Priest underbinds on the right,
C- but the Scholar overbinds the Priest on the right.

Figures 4.43
(Continued from previous page)
D- The Priest answers by rotating his sword up
and to the right,
E- continuing to rotate his sword and buckler,
F- overbinding the Scholar on the left,
G- he binds with his buckler,
H- and Nuckens.

Another option for the Priest in Underarm, although not a very safe one, is to grab the Scholar's sword. He does this by taking his own sword blade in his left hand and freeing his right hand, which is concealed behind his buckler.

The Priest then reaches forward with his right hand and grasps the Scholar's sword. His aim is to enter as rapidly as possible to stab the Scholar with the sword in his left hand.

Figures 4.44
A- The Priest in Underarm, the Scholar in Longpoint.
B- The Priest grabs the Scholar's sword,
C- Raising his own to strike,
D- he thrusts to the Scholar's chest.

However, there is a very simple counter to the Priest's action. The Scholar passes forward and Shield-Knocks the Priest's hand while pulling his sword away. The Priest will be unable to hold onto the sword. It is interesting that the author of I.33 states that the Scholar's sword "cannot be freed except through a Shield-Strike [Shield-Knock]."[27] Experimentation with sharp swords shows that a stationary sword can indeed be grabbed and held without injury, particularly by a gloved hand.

Once the Scholar's blade is free, he may respond in either of two ways. Firstly he may thrust, which is what the Priest advises. Secondly, he may cut at the Priest's head. The Priest can defend against a cut with the sword and buckler held in his left hand. Once the Priest has parried the cut he can pass forward, grappling the Scholar's extended arms from above and using the sword in his left hand to thrust the Scholar in the body as he does so.

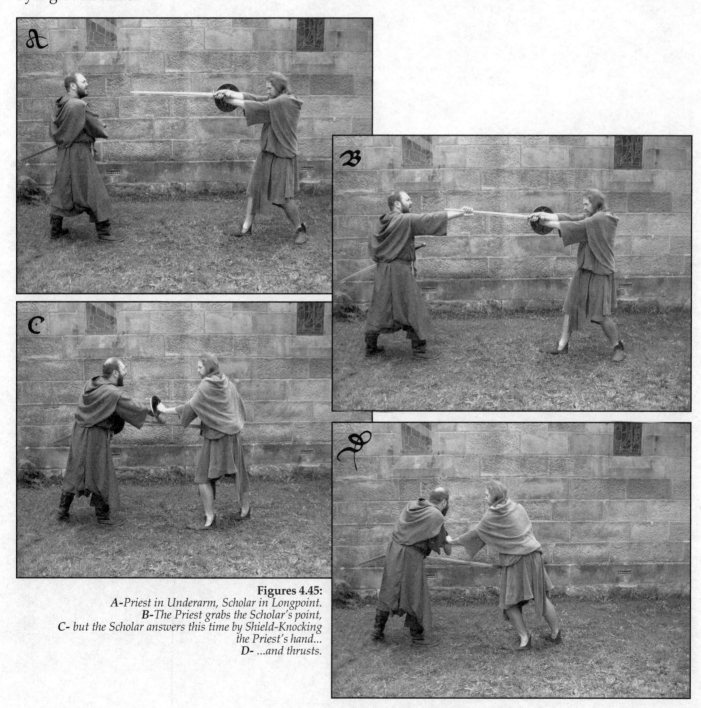

Figures 4.45:
A-Priest in Underarm, Scholar in Longpoint.
B-The Priest grabs the Scholar's point,
C- but the Scholar answers this time by Shield-Knocking
the Priest's hand...
D- ...and thrusts.

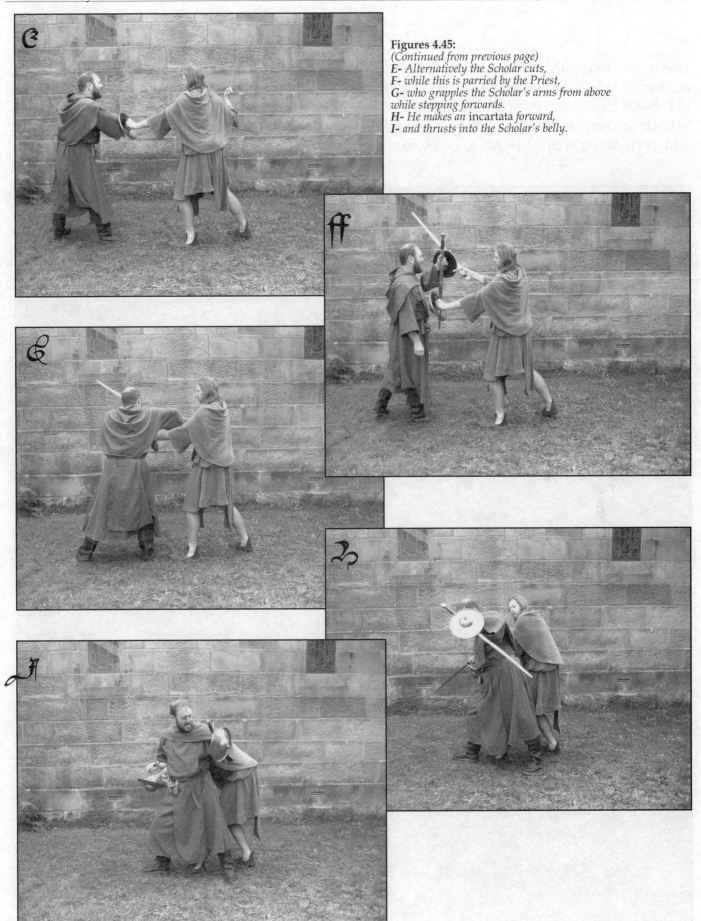

Figures 4.45:
(Continued from previous page)
E- Alternatively the Scholar cuts,
F- while this is parried by the Priest,
G- who grapples the Scholar's arms from above while stepping forwards.
H- He makes an incartata *forward,*
I- and thrusts into the Scholar's belly.

OTHER COUNTERS

There are two other counters to Underarm, neither of which is illustrated in I.33. The first of these is Underarm itself. From Underarm the Scholar can respond to any attack by overbinding and performing a Shield-Knock, or by moving into the Crutch, parrying and grappling. Once the Scholar has either moved to overbind or entered the Crutch, he is in a position described above and everything follows as it has already been described.

Figures 4.46
A-Priest and Scholar both in Underarm.
B-The Priest attacks with an Unterhau at the Scholar's head.
C- In answer the Scholar overbinds on the right,
D- Shield-Knocks,
E- and cuts to the Priest's head.

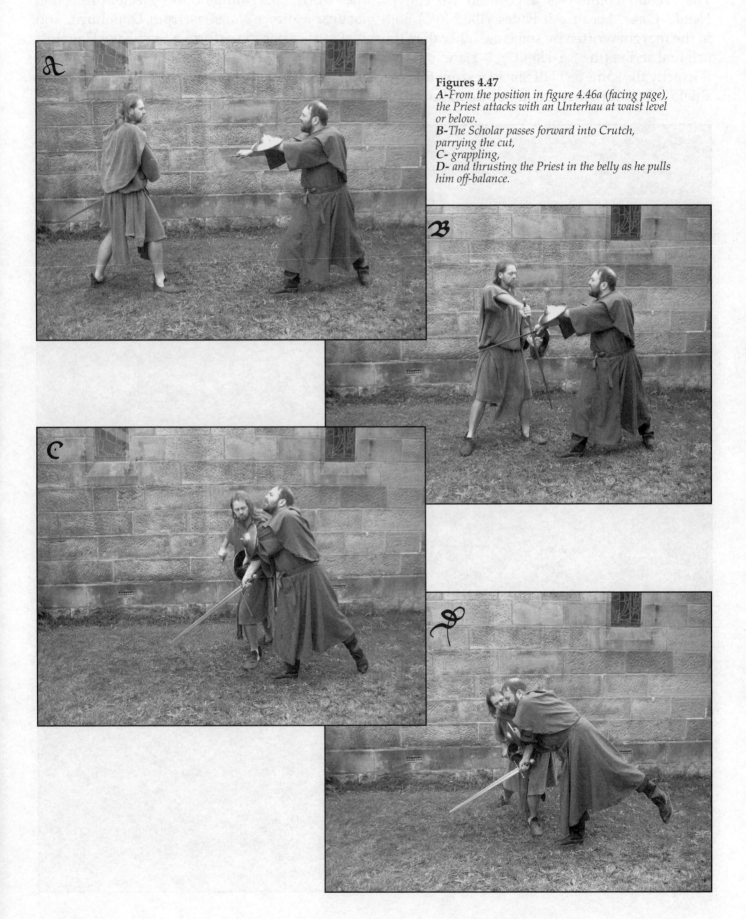

Figures 4.47
A-From the position in figure 4.46a (facing page), the Priest attacks with an Unterhau at waist level or below.
B-The Scholar passes forward into Crutch, parrying the cut,
C- grappling,
D- and thrusting the Priest in the belly as he pulls him off-balance.

The second counter is a position we call *B-Hand's Cover*, because it is described by a note in the margin written by someone other than the original scribe (the "A-Hand"). B-Hand's Cover is exactly the same as Half Shield, except that the shield is held to the right, rather than the left, of the sword. This counter offers greater protection against a direct *Unterhau* from Underarm, and makes it easier to perform a Stab-Knock against this simple attack. Apart from that it functions identically to Half Shield.

Figures 4.48
A-Priest in Underarm, Scholar in B-Hand's cover.
B-The Priest attacks with an Unterhau *and the Scholar Stab-Knocks.*
C- However, the Priest may fall under the sword, overbind,
D- and Shield-Knock.

SUMMARY

The play between Underarm and its counters forms the core of the I.33 system of sword and buckler, which is why this chapter is the longest and most complex in the book. Mastery of falling under the sword, and the various sequences that follow from that, is absolutely essential. As we will see in the following chapters, many other wards and counters are used, but as the author of I.33 points out, "all of this can be reduced to the first guard and the opposition called Half Shield etc.."[28]

⸰ NOTES ⸰

[1] Jeffrey L. Forgeng, *The Art of Medieval Swordsmanship*: *A Facsimile and Translation of Europe's Oldest Personal Combat Treatise, Royal Armouries MS.I.33,* Union City, 2003, Plate 49.

[2] I.33 shows one instance of falling under the sword from Left Shoulder, which will be described in Chapter 6.

[3] For example, Fiore Dei Liberi, *Il Fior di Battaglia*, Italy, 1409 (MS Ludwig XV.13, Getty Museum, Los Angeles), Plate 20R

[4] Forgeng, 2003, Plate 3.

[5] For example, if the Priest adopts *vom Tag*, the Scholar counters with Half Shield, the Priest may well choose to "counter" Half Shield with Underarm; see Chapter 7.

[6] In much the same way that the German longsword master Liechtenauer's *Meisterhau* each "counter" one of the guard positions. "The first strike is the *Krumphau*. It counters *Ochs*. The second strike is the *Zwerchau*. It counters *vom Tag*. The third strike is the *Schielhau*. It counters *Pflug*. The fourth strike is the *Scheitelhau*. It counters *Alber*." Sigmund Ringeck, quoted and translated in Christian Tobler, *Secrets of German Medieval Swordsmanship,* Union City, 2001, p. 84.

[7] Forgeng, 2003, Plate 3.

[8] Ibid.

[9] This technique is described in the manuscript as part of the encounter between Underarm and the Priest's Special Longpoint (Plate 47). However, it proceeds from the same bind as used in the Shield-Knock, and is an appropriate response when facing Half Shield.

[10] Forgeng, 2003, Plate 49.

[11] This technique is described in the manuscript as part of the encounter between Underarm and the Priest's Special Longpoint (Plate 49). However, it proceeds from the same bind as used in the Shield-Knock, and is an appropriate response when facing Half Shield.

[12] Forgeng, 2003, Plate 4 "note also that the Student has nothing he can do but Shield-Strike or to use his left hand to envelop the Priest's arms"

[13] Ibid.

[14] Ibid. Plate 6.

[15] Ibid. Plate 7.

[16] This technique is described in the manuscript as part of the encounter between Underarm and Longpoint (Plate 36). However, it proceeds from the same bind as used in the Shield-Knock, and on Plate 4 the author of I.33 notes that seizing the binder's sword and shield in the right arm is an appropriate response when facing Half Shield.

[17] This technique is described in the manuscript as part of the encounter between Underarm and Longpoint (Plate 14 and 15). However, it proceeds from the same bind as used in the Shield-Knock, and is an appropriate response.

[18] Forgeng, 2003, Plate 8.

[19] Ibid. Plate 40.

[20] In defence of this view, when describing cutting swords with about as much weight and impetus, the 19th century writer, John Taylor stated, that "in striking at his leg, your head and sword arm must become exposed even to a person wholly ignorant of the science; and his attention not being occupied by endeavouring to parry, his blow at the head would probably prove fatal, even though he received a cut on the leg" John Taylor, *The Art of Defence on Foot with the Broad Sword and Sabre: adapted also to the Spadroon, or Cut-and-Thrust Sword,* 1804, p 89.

[21] Note that the sword is shown somewhat higher than this in the manuscript. The authors prefer the hilt lower for several reasons. A higher hilt (and particularly a higher buckler) obscures the vision. It makes the arm more vulnerable to a direct cut and paradoxically, by forcing the defender to drop the forte of the blade when parrying, makes the head vulnerable to attacks initiated with low feints.

[22] *Winden* or "winding" is a technique widely used in German longsword systems where the orientation of the hands, and therefore of the sword, is changed to gain greater leverage over an opposing blade. However, *wind* is also used to describe the simple rotation of the hand when using short single weapons. For example, *Codex Wallerstein* describes the rotation of the *messer* from a low ward to a hanging ward in preparation to parry as "if anyone strikes downward at your head, wind under past him with your falchion and receive the stroke on it" Grzegorz Zabinski and Bartlomiei Walczak, *Codex Wallerstein,* Boulder, 2002 p.128.

[23] Forgeng, 2003, Plate 8.

[24] Ibid. Plate 2.

[25] Ibid. Plate 31.

[26] Ibid. Plate 12.

[27] Ibid. Plate 32.

[28] Ibid. Plate 49 L.

CHAPTER 5
THE SECOND WARD "RIGHT SHOULDER"

The Second Ward in I.33 is *Right Shoulder*. The sword is held sloped back on the right shoulder and the buckler is extended in front of the body, face towards the opponent. The left leg is forward.

Right Shoulder is adopted in order to launch powerful forehand attacks. The obvious attack from Right Shoulder is the right *Oberhau*, a diagonally descending blow from right to left, but vertical and horizontal attacks from the right can be made from this ward as well as diagonally descending *Oberhau* from the left (although these are less natural). Most attacks will be accompanied by a slope pace forward and right. This carries the attacker around to the left side of an opponent where it can be difficult for him to judge the exact height of the attack in order to make a buckler parry. In addition an attacker may Shield-Knock, that is he may deflect a defending buckler with his own. Figures 5.2 show an attack against a generic ward.

Figure 5.1
Right Shoulder Ward

Figures 5.2
A- *The Priest in Right Shoulder, the Scholar in a low ward with the buckler extended.*
B- *The Priest attacks using a Shield-Knock,*
C- *striking the Scholar with a right Oberhau*

THE FIRST COUNTER: RIGHT COVER

I.33 describes two counters against Right Shoulder. The first is Right Cover which is held with the left foot forward. The sword and buckler are held on the right side of the body with the buckler facing to the right, apparently exposing the left side to the obvious attack of an *Oberhau*.

As with any deliberate invitation in fencing, this is an attempt to sucker the opponent into attacking the obvious opening. If the obvious attack is made, the Scholar winds clockwise, bringing his buckler around to face to the left. He simultaneously makes a slope pace forward and right (more right than forward) and thrusts his point into the attacker's face while parrying the cut with the buckler. This technique is a Stab-Knock.

Figure 5.3 *The first counter, Right Cover, from the front and side.*

If the Priest does not attack he suffers the same fate. The Scholar again makes a slope pace forward and right (this time more forward than right), thrusting his point into the stationary Priest's face.

Figures 5.4
A- *The Priest in Right Shoulder, the Scholar in Right Cover.*
B- *The Priest attacks with an Oberhau.*
C- *In response the Scholar slope paces right and thrusts at the Priest's face.*

Alternatively, from fig. A
D- *If the Priest does not attack immediately, the Scholar attacks the stationary Priest with a thrust delivered on a slope pace forward and right.*

The Priest in Right Shoulder is unable to attack the Scholar in Right Cover, so therefore he must try another approach. The Scholar's blade is extended, so the Priest will bind with the sword. The Priest should pass forward, binding the Scholar's sword with his own. The bind created by the Priest is almost symmetrical. The Priest is right leg forward and the Scholar left leg forward.

Figures 5.5
A- The Priest in Right Shoulder, the Scholar in Right Cover.
B- The Priest now binds the Scholar's blade, then immediately passes forward.

However, passing forward and binding without creating any threat does not place the Scholar under any pressure. The Scholar may easily respond with a ceding parry as described at 5.9. In order to be more effective, the Priest should commence the obvious attack, a right *Oberhau*. The Scholar will respond as at 5.4, by slipping right and thrusting to the Priest's face. As the Scholar commences his counterattack, the Priest will abort his attack, instead binding the Scholar's blade. Unlike the bind created at 5.6, this bind is asymmetrical and the Priest finishes the action with a *nucken*.

Figures 5.6
A- The Priest in Right Shoulder, the Scholar in Right Cover.
B- The Priest passes forward cutting with an Oberhau.
C- The Scholar responds by slope pacing forward, thrusting at the Priest.
D- The Priest now aborts his cut and binds instead.
E- The Priest binds buckler to buckler,
F- and Nuckens.

From the symmetrical bind created at 5.6 the Priest has the initiative. However, the author of I.33 notes that the Priest and the Scholar can both perform the same actions. Indeed it is the Scholar who is shown performing them. The first possible action is to press the opposing sword down to the left and to Tread Through. The Scholar presses the Priest's sword down while passing forward. He then binds the Priest's sword and buckler with his own, and cuts up at the Priest's head with a *nucken*.

Figures 5.7
A- The Priest and Scholar are bound as in fig. 5.5.
B- This time the Scholar presses the Priest's sword down, passing forward and binding with the buckler,
C- and cuts up at the Priest's head with a
Nucken.

The Priest can respond to the Tread-Through by ceding with the Scholar's pressure. As the Scholar presses the Priest's sword to the latter's right, the Priest does not resist the pressure. He rotates his sword hand clockwise, moving it up and to the right and letting his point sink under the Scholar's blade. The Priest then presses the Scholar's blade out to his right. Once the ceding parry is complete, the Priest should cut with an *Oberhau* to the Scholar's head, while pressing down on his sword arm with his buckler. Alternatively, the Priest may disengage under the Scholar's bind, thrusting him in the belly. However, this can be risky, as it relies on speed, not on controlling the Scholar's blade. Therefore in an extension of this technique, the Priest can change sword, rotating his blade through 360 degrees and overbinding the Scholar on the right, from which the Shield-Knock obviously follows.

Figures 5.8
Again from the bind in fig. 5.5.
A- The Scholar overbinds to the left and the Priest makes a ceding parry.
B- The completion of the ceding parry.
C- The riposte with a Shield-Knock.
(continued on p. 162)

Figure 5.9
(continued from p. 161)
A- *As an alternative to the last play (p. 161), as the Scholar overbinds the Priest cedes,*
B- *and thrusts to the Scholar's belly or chest.*
C- *Another, safer alternative is for the Priest to cede, rotating his sword clockwise,*
D- *changing sword and overbinding on the right from where he can Shield-Knock.*

Should the Priest make his ceding parry (particularly the variant shown at 5.9c and d), the Scholar's only defence is to Stab-Knock. He rotates his sword hand clockwise, binding the Priest's buckler with his own as he makes a slope pace forward and left (more left than forward) and thrusts at the Priest's face.

Figures 5.10
A- Now bound as in fig. 5.5, the Scholar overbinds to the left and the Priest makes a ceding parry.
B- But the Scholar strikes the Priest with a Stab-Knock.

If we now move back to the initial bind we will see the other options that the Scholar has once he is bound by the Priest. The Scholar can cut directly from the bind. He may cut on the left, which the author of I.33 says is what common fencers do, or on the right, which the author of I.33 tells us is what he and his students do. In the attack on the left the Scholar rotates his hand counter clockwise, changing his sword from the inside to the outside of the Priest's, and cutting down into the Priest's arms or head. As he does this he steps forward and left. The Scholar makes the attack on the right by slope pacing forward and right, rotating his sword hand counterclockwise and cutting to the Priest's face. The slope pace forward and right creates the angle the Scholar needs to make this attack.

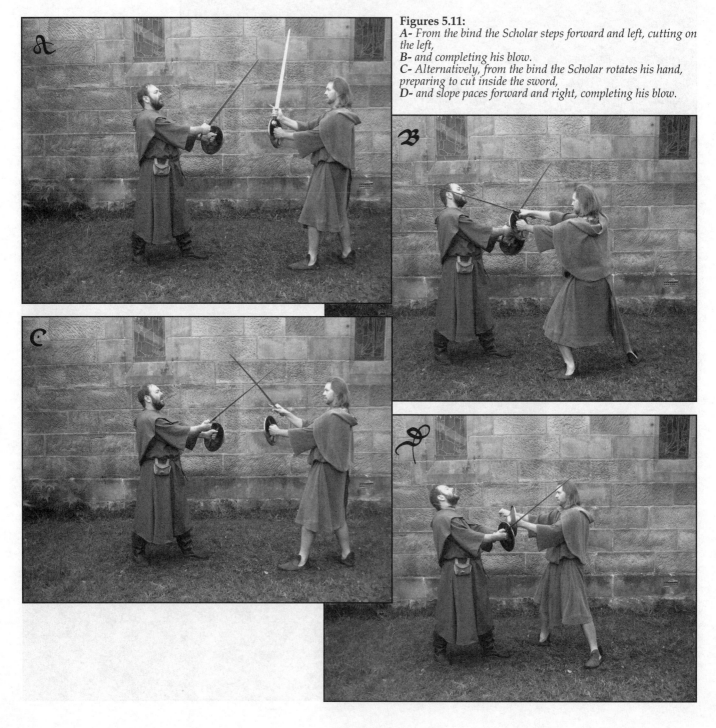

Figures 5.11:
A- From the bind the Scholar steps forward and left, cutting on the left,
B- and completing his blow.
C- Alternatively, from the bind the Scholar rotates his hand, preparing to cut inside the sword,
D- and slope paces forward and right, completing his blow.

Either of the above attacks may be countered by the Priest sticking to the Scholar's sword and attacking straight down into the Scholar's hands. Sticking to the Scholar's sword means the Priest cuts into the Scholar's blade at a sharp angle and slides his blade down the Scholar's, allowing the Scholar's blade to direct the Priest's into the former's hands. Against a cut to the left the Priest's countercut is made towards the right. Against the cut to his right the Priest's countercut is made towards his left.

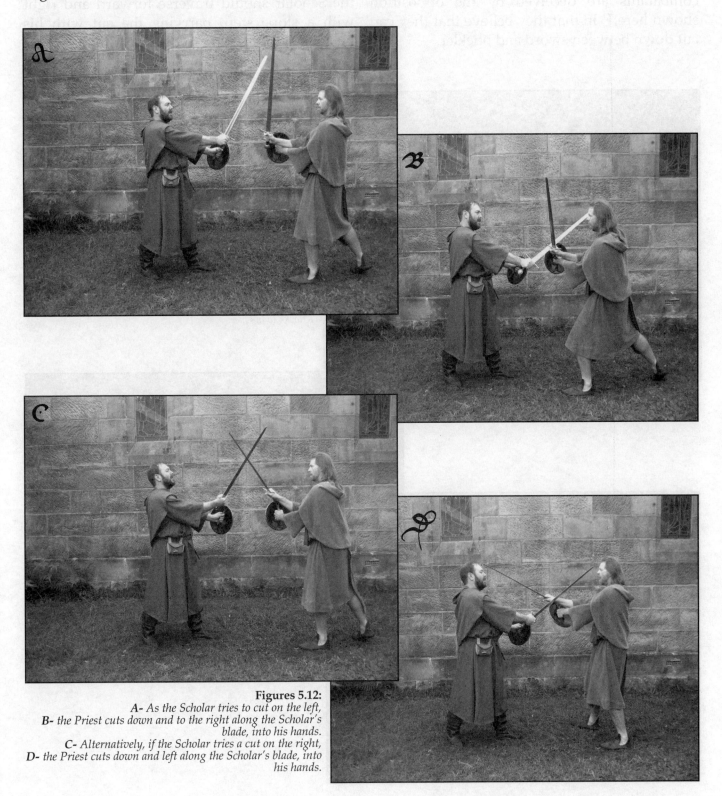

Figures 5.12:
A- As the Scholar tries to cut on the left,
B- the Priest cuts down and to the right along the Scholar's blade, into his hands.
C- Alternatively, if the Scholar tries a cut on the right,
D- the Priest cuts down and left along the Scholar's blade, into his hands.

THE SECOND COUNTER: HALF SHIELD

The author of I.33 describes a second counter to the ward of Right Shoulder. This is Half Shield. Only one attack is described against Half Shield, and it states in I.33 that "many common combatants are deceived by the opposition shown here,"[1] in that they believe that they can cut down between sword and buckler.

This is another attempt to sucker the opponent into making an obvious attack and is particularly effective if the sword and buckler are held invitingly apart. If the Priest makes this attack, the Scholar should traverse forward and right with a slope step, parrying the cut with his buckler and thrusting to the Priest's face with a Stab-Knock.

Figures 5.13
A- The Priest in Right Shoulder, the Scholar counters with Half Shield.
B- The Priest cuts down between the sword and shield.
C- But the Scholar slope steps right and Stab-Knocks to his face.

This sequence is a good example of where the author of I.33 has not provided us with a complete system. Half Shield is not fully explored as a counter to Right Shoulder; rather it feels as if the author of I.33 liked the above counterattack so much that he simply had to include it. However, if Half Shield follows the pattern of other counters, the Scholar should also have offensive capabilities if the Priest does not attack.

In cases such as this it is left to modern interpreters to "fill in the gaps," using the principles and models outlined elsewhere in the manuscript. One possibility here is for the Scholar to pass forward and left, passing his sword underneath his shield to deliver a thrust into the Priest's face while binding bucklers; the line of the attack cuts off the Priest's main attack, and threatens his arm as he strikes.

Figures 5.14
A- *From the position in 5.13a (facing page), the Scholar passes in and left, thrusting to the Priest's face.*
B- *Alternatively, if the Priest cuts with a right Oberhau, the Scholar makes the same attack, closing off the Priest's line of attack.*

There are, unfortunately, many such omissions in I.33. In this book we have offered a number of extrapolations that we feel are both obvious and important for an understanding of the style, but the reader is encouraged to explore other possibilities themselves, once the principles of the manuscript have been mastered.

[1] Jeffrey L. Forgeng, *The Art of Medieval Swordsmanship*: *A Facsimile and Translation of Europe's Oldest Personal Combat Treatise, Royal Armouries MS. I.33*, Union City 2003, Plate 21U.

Figure 6.1 *Left Shoulder.*

CHAPTER 6
THE THIRD WARD "LEFT SHOULDER"

The third ward in I.33 is *Left Shoulder*. The sword is held sloped back and slightly upwards over the left shoulder, the buckler is held in front of the body, face towards the opponent and the right leg is forward.

Left Shoulder is adopted in order to launch powerful attacks from the left. The natural attack is an *Oberhau*, a cut diagonally down from left to right. Because of the position of the left arm, it is impossible to cut from the left below about shoulder height without withdrawing the buckler. This would leave the forearm exposed to a countercut and hence is not an option. Other attacks that can be made from Left Shoulder are horizontal cuts to the right side of the opponent's head, descending vertical cuts and cuts to the left side of the body. These latter are slower than the corresponding cuts from Right Shoulder because the blade must travel further. However, it should be borne in mind that a slow attack is not necessarily a bad one. All attacks from Left Shoulder must commence by raising the hand. At this point it is impossible to know what attack is being made. A cunning attacker will not even decide himself which attack he will make until he sees the response of his opponent, much as we have already seen when falling under the sword from Underarm. As the hand continues to raise, it will become apparent that the attack is not a left *Oberhau* but it could still be any of the other cuts described. Further movement of the hand reveals that the attack is not going to be a vertically descending *Scheitelhau*. It could, however, still be a right *Oberhau* or a horizontal *Mittelhau*. Finally the attack continues around in an arc and becomes a *Mittelhau*, a cross-strike from right to left. Only as this is about to land can the defender be sure of what attack his opponent is making.

The sequence below shows the effectiveness of such an attack against a typical stance used by a fencer unfamiliar with the I.33 system. As the attack commences, the defender presents his blade against it. This is avoided. If the defender then tries to parry with his buckler, this too can be avoided, resulting in a cut delivered under the buckler.

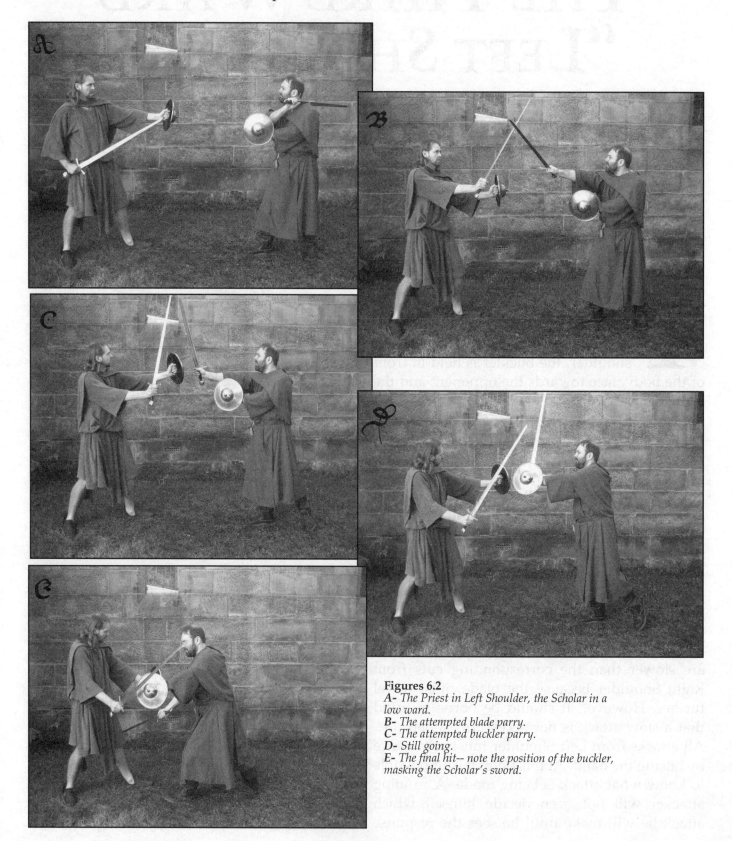

Figures 6.2
A- The Priest in Left Shoulder, the Scholar in a low ward.
B- The attempted blade parry.
C- The attempted buckler parry.
D- Still going.
E- The final hit-- note the position of the buckler, masking the Scholar's sword.

THE FIRST COUNTER - LEFT COVER

I.33 describes three counters against Left Shoulder. The first of these is Left Cover which is similar to the Crutch. Left Cover is held with the right foot forward and the hilt high, with the blade hanging towards the ground. The buckler is facing to the right and passed under the sword hand to the right of the blade. The sword and buckler are held on the left side of the body

In similar fashion to Right Cover against Right Shoulder, this apparently leaves the Scholar open to the most obvious attack from Left Shoulder, the left *Oberhau*. Again, as with Right Shoulder and Right Cover, this is a lure. If the Priest makes the obvious left *Oberhau*, the Scholar passes forward and left with the left leg (more left than forward), rotating the hand clockwise and delivers a Stab-Knock to the Priest's face.

Figures 6.2 *The first counter - Left Cover*

Figures 6.4
*A- The Priest in Left Shoulder, the Scholar in Left
Cover.*
B- The Priest makes a left Oberhau,
*C- but here the Scholar traverses left and Stab-
Knocks.*

This same action is used if the Priest makes no attack. The Scholar passes forward and left (this time more forward than left), rotating the hands clockwise and thrusting to the Priest's face, or anticlockwise and thrusting to his belly.

Figures 6.5
(from 6.4a, facing page)
A- The Scholar attacks this time, because the Priest is stationary, with a thrust to the face.
B- Another option would be to attack the belly directly with a thrust.

If the Priest attempts a *Scheitelhau*, the Scholar can respond as he did at figure 6.5, with a Stab-Knock. If the Priest continues his blade around to attack the Scholar's left side then he is attacking into a formed ward, an action which is inadvisable, particularly as the Priest is passing forward with his left leg while cutting from the right, an inherently weak attack. The Scholar can either intercept the Priest's blade early, performing a Stab-Knock as at figure 6.4 or may remain in his ward, parrying as in figure 6.6. If the Scholar parries, he can perform a Shield-Knock, rotating his sword hand and delivering a right *Oberhau* to the Priest's head or left side.

Figures 6.6
A- The Priest in Left Shoulder, the Scholar
in Left Cover.
B- The Priest attacks with a right *Oberhau*,
and the Scholar parries.
C- The Scholar ripostes with a Shield-Knock
and a right *Oberhau*.

With Left Cover neutralizing all potential attacks from Left Shoulder, the Priest must instead bind the Scholar's blade. The Priest winds clockwise, overbinding the Scholar's blade on the right. This may seem to be a very similar action to the direct attack described above, but is actually quite different as the Scholar is not passing forward and the speed of his hand action is not tied to the speed of his foot. The Priest will also be out of range of the Scholar at the end of the action.

From the overbind the Priest may perform a Shield-Knock as shown in earlier chapters. As he binds he will pass forward, binding with the buckler and following this up with a cut to the Scholar's head.

Figure 6.7a *The Priest in Left Shoulder, the Scholar in Left Cover.*

Figure 6.7b *The Priest binds...*

Figure 6.7c *...Shield-Knocks...*

Figure 6.7d *...and winds up to deliver a powerful blow.*

As the Priest overbinds him, the Scholar should wind clockwise, so that he is in a position like those in earlier overbinds. From this position the Priest can perform any of the actions described in Chapter 4 in response to a Shield-Knock.

Figures 6.8
A- From the position in 6.7a, the Priest binds.
B- As the Priest binds, the Scholar rotates his hands,
C- and returns the favor, binding the Priest.
D- He is now free to Shield-Knock.

Alternatively the Scholar may leave his hands as they are. He should pass forward and left, sliding his blade upwards to free it from the bind while using his buckler arm to envelop the Priest's arms and wrap them into his body. The Scholar may now break the Priest's arms or simply strike the Priest with his sword.

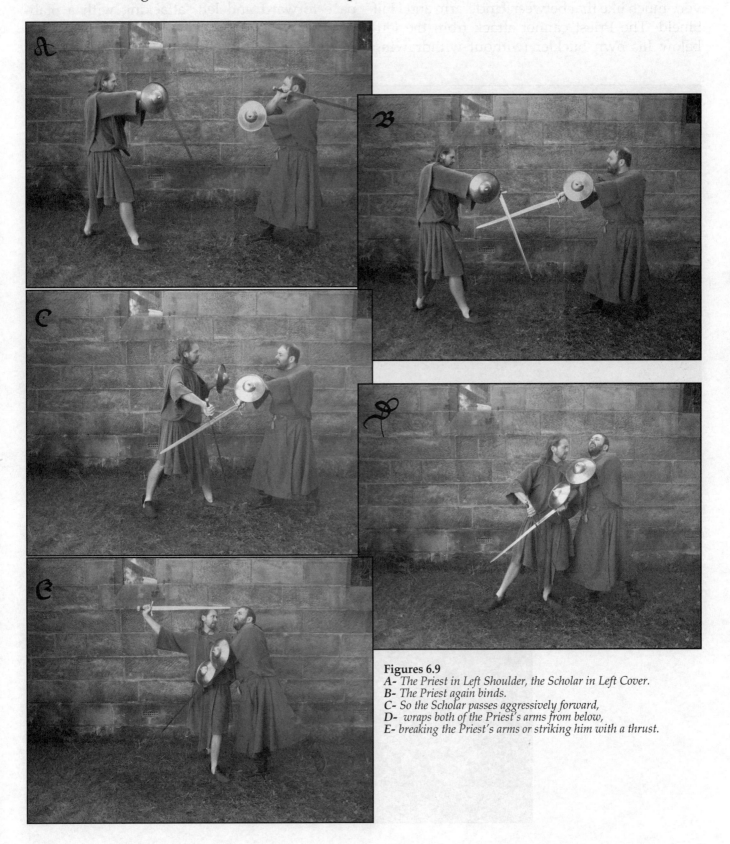

Figures 6.9
A- *The Priest in Left Shoulder, the Scholar in Left Cover.*
B- *The Priest again binds.*
C- *So the Scholar passes aggressively forward,*
D- *wraps both of the Priest's arms from below,*
E- *breaking the Priest's arms or striking him with a thrust.*

THE SECOND COUNTER ⁃ HALF SHIELD

The second counter for Left Shoulder described in I.33 is Half Shield. This results in a situation very much like that between Underarm and Half Shield. The Priest cannot attack from the left, below his own buckler (without withdrawing his buckler and exposing his arm). If he attacks with a left *Oberhau* the Scholar can make a slope pace forward and left, attacking with a Stab-Knock.

Figures 6.10
A- The Priest in Left Shoulder, the Scholar in Half Shield.
B- The Priest makes a left Oberhau, *while the Scholar Stab-Knocks.*

Therefore the Priest's best option, as in Underarm, is to fall under the sword. He takes a small step forward and right while extending his sword and underbinding the Scholar on the right. From this position the author of I.33 states, "you have here all the actions of the first guard, or Under-Arm."[1]

The Scholar responds to the Priest falling under the sword by overbinding on the right, advancing and performing a Shield-Knock. The Priest can obviously respond with any of the responses to a Shield-Knock shown in Chapter 4, change of sword, tread through, etc..

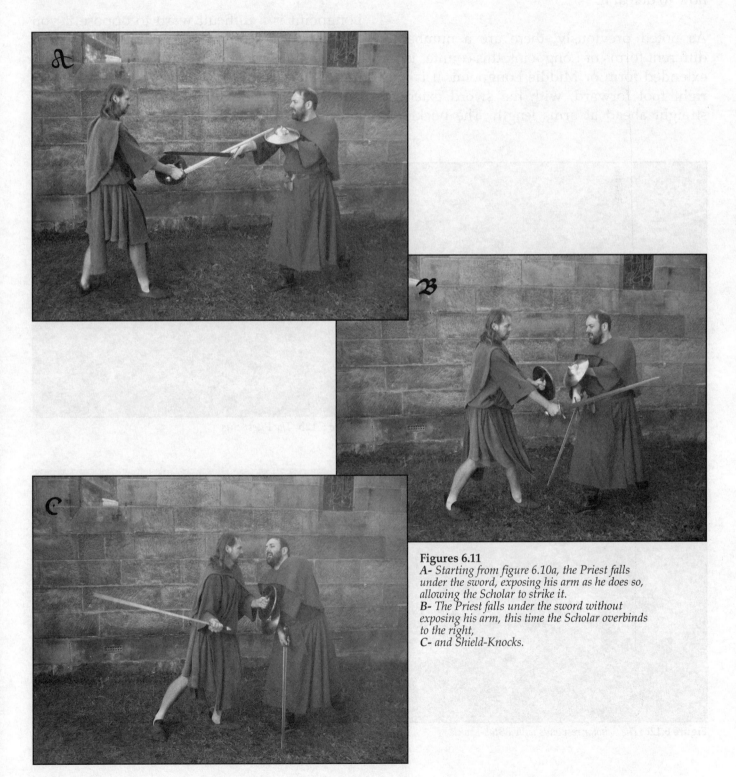

Figures 6.11
A- Starting from figure 6.10a, the Priest falls under the sword, exposing his arm as he does so, allowing the Scholar to strike it.
B- The Priest falls under the sword without exposing his arm, this time the Scholar overbinds to the right,
C- and Shield-Knocks.

THE THIRD COUNTER · LONGPOINT

The author of I.33 now introduces a third counter, Longpoint, which he says "all common fencers use." It is clear that he does not favour this counter, but shows it in order to describe how to defeat it.

As noted previously, there are a number of different forms of Longpoint; this counter is the extended form or Middle Longpoint. It is held right foot forward, with the sword extended straight ahead at arms length. The buckler is generally held passed underneath the forearm to the right of the blade. This position allows the sword arm to be rested on the shield arm, and helps maintain what is otherwise a tiring ward.

Longpoint is a difficult ward to oppose if you don't know the correct method. If the Priest does nothing, the Scholar can simply thrust into him. If the Priest makes any sort of attack, the Scholar can make a slope pace forward and left and deliver a Stab-Knock.

Figure 6.12a *The Priest in Left Shoulder, the Scholar in Extended Longpoint.*

Figure 6.12b *The Priest cuts.*

Figure 6.12c *The Scholar responds with a Stab-Knock.*

Figure 6.12d *Alternatively, if the Priest is stationary, the Scholar could also thrust.*

The weakness of Longpoint is that it is vulnerable to being bound. The Priest states that "the counters to this opposition are two bindings, of which one is on the right above the sword, the other on the left."[2] The first of these is the more effective and unless the Scholar is deliberately trying to avoid it by holding his sword over to his right, it is the only bind possible. From this bind the Priest can advance and Shield-Knock.

Figures 6.13
A- The Priest in Left Shoulder, the Scholar in Middle Longpoint.
B- Taking advantage of the innate weakness of Longpoint, the Priest overbinds on the right,
C- advances and Shield-Knocks.

183

Once again, as the Priest attempts the Shield-Knock, the Scholar is able to respond with any of the techniques described in Chapter 4.

If the Scholar tries to avoid being overbound on the right by holding his sword well across to

his right the Priest can respond by overbinding him on the left. The Priest can then advance and Shield-Knock, cutting upwards into the Scholar's face with a *nucken*.

Figures 6.14
A- The Priest in Left Shoulder, the Scholar in Middle Longpoint, trying to avoid an overbind on the right by holding his sword a bit more to the right.
B- So the Priest overbinds on the left...

Figures 6.14
C- ...advances, Shield-Knocks,
D- and delivers a Nucken.

⸙ NOTES ⸙

[1] Jeffrey L. Forgeng, **The Art of Medieval Swordsmanship**: *A Facsimile & Translation of Europe's Oldest Personal Combat Treatise, Royal Armouries MS I.33*, Union City, 2003, Plate 26 U.

[2] Ibid. Plate 27 L.

CHAPTER 7

THE FOURTH WARD
"VOM TAG"

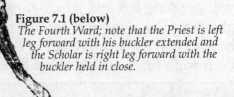

Figure 7.1 (below)
The Fourth Ward; note that the Priest is left leg forward with his buckler extended and the Scholar is right leg forward with the buckler held in close.

The fourth ward is not given a name in I.33, but it is a common enough stance in medieval *fechtbücher* which name it *vom Tag* ("from the roof"). *Vom Tag* can launch powerful *Oberhäue* from the left or right, as with the Right and Left Shoulder wards, but the fastest attack is a *Scheitelhau*, a cut directly down onto the head on a pass forward.

Vom Tag can be held either foot forward, although in I.33 the right foot forward is perhaps more typical. The sword is held with the hilt raised above the head, with the point sloping backwards, anywhere from slightly above horizontal to sloping down towards the ground. The buckler can be held facing forward, facing left, or facing right; when left leg forward, it is best held extended and facing to the left, and when right leg forward it is best held facing right, covering the right armpit.

I.33 provides three possible counters to *vom Tag*: Underarm, the Priest's Special Longpoint, and Half Shield. The Priest's Special Longpoint is covered in detail in Chapter 11, so here we will look only at Underarm and Half Shield.

The First Counter - Underarm

Underarm is actually the second Counter to *vom Tag*, but is described here first because it introduces the important concept of *High Cover*.

Having adopted Underarm, the Scholar can defend himself from any attack as outlined in Figures 4.2 and 4.3; that is, by passing forward and left and lifting his sword to deflect any incoming attack. However, the Scholar need not wait to be attacked, but can use this same movement to immediately offend the Priest. We call the transitional position he passes into *High Cover*.

Having countered the Priest's *vom Tag* by adopting Underarm, the Scholar immediately swings his sword upward so his hilt is above eye level, stepping left and a little forward with the right foot. The right arm should be bent at the elbow so that the sword blade is on his left-hand side (inside line), and his buckler should be to the left of his sword-hand. This covering is very similar to falling under the sword, except that the blade is sloping and the point is low, making it difficult for the Priest to overbind.

If the Priest does nothing, the Scholar can continue his movement by passing forward and left with the left foot, separating sword and buckler and cutting forcefully upwards into the Priest's sword arm. As he does this the Scholar binds the Priest's buckler with his own, preventing any buckler parry. If the Priest retreats, the Scholar can pass forward and thrust into the Priest's breast. If the Priest panics and strikes into the ward, the Scholar can parry and perform the variation of the Shield-Knock described in Figures 4.2 and 4.3; bind or stop the attacking sword with his own sword, then sweep the Priest's sword and buckler away to the left with his own buckler while uncrossing and striking the Priest's head.

Figures 7.2
A- The Priest adopts vom Tag, *the Scholar Underarm.*
B- The Scholar adopts High Cover
C- and strikes at the Priest's sword arm,
D- but the Priest retreats; the Scholar thrusts into the Priest's breast.
E- Alternatively, starting from the image in Fig. 7.2b, the Priest strikes an Oberhau, which the Scholar parries.
F- The Scholar Shield-Knocks,
G- and strikes the Priest.

The Priest has one more response to an attack from High Cover, an attempt to bind the Scholar's sword and buckler and countercut to the side of the Scholar's head.

Figures 7.3
A- The Priest in vom Tag, the Scholar in Underarm.
B- The Scholar executes a High Cover.
C- The Priest binds with his buckler,
D- and passes forward and right with a strike to the Scholar's head.

The Scholar's response to this attack is a special form of thrust, the thrust from the left described in Chapter 3. If the Priest attacks the Scholar in High Cover, either by binding with the buckler or cutting down on the Scholar's exposed sword-arm, the Scholar simply passes circularly forward and left, rotating his sword-and-buckler clockwise to bring his point on line to the opponent's face. His buckler will deflect the blow and/or prevent the bind. This is a Stab-Knock.

The Priest's best response to the Scholar's adoption of Underarm is to abandon *vom Tag* entirely and move into an appropriate counter of his own, Half Shield, returning to a familiar position from which we already know how to proceed. The lack of a response from *vom Tag* to the Scholar in Underarm suggests that *vom Tag* is not a ward favoured by the author of I.33.

Figure 7.4a *From the position in 7.3a (facing page), the Priest binds bucklers and prepares to pass forward with his cut.*

Figure 7.4b *The Scholar rotates his weapons and executes a thrust from the left on a half incartata.*

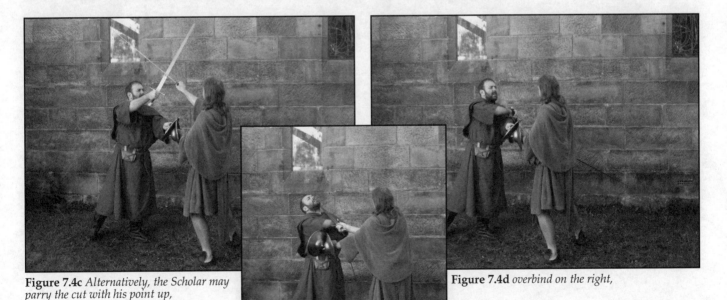

Figure 7.4c *Alternatively, the Scholar may parry the cut with his point up,*

Figure 7.4d *overbind on the right,*

Figure 7.4e *and complete a Shield-Knock.*

THE SECOND COUNTER · HALF SHIELD

The other counter to *vom Tag* is Half Shield. If attacked while in Half Shield, the Scholar should use the defensive Stab-Knocks already seen in Fig. 3.10, 3.11 and 3.12. If the attack is to the Scholar's left side, he should pass forward and left, Stab-Knocking to the Priest's belly. If the attack is to the Scholar's right side, he should traverse left, Stab-Knocking to the Priest's face. If the attack is vertical, either of these will be effective.

I.33 does not indicate if Half Shield can enter against *vom Tag*, but there would seem to be no reason why the Scholar could not pass into High Cover from Half Shield as well as from Underarm. The only difference is that as the sword and buckler are wound upwards into High Cover the buckler ends up on the right of the sword. Otherwise the play is identical to that shown above.

Figures 7.5
A- The Scholar is in Half Shield, the Priest in vom Tag.

B- The Scholar enters against vom Tag.

CHAPTER 8

THE SIXTH WARD "PFLUG"

What happened to the Fifth Ward? Like the author of I.33, the current authors have decided to place the Sixth Ward before the Fifth, which we believe is where it best fits. The fact that Sixth Ward is shown first is logical in terms of teaching the skills needed to fence in the I.33 system. It is used to deliver only one attack, the thrust from the left. This is the primary attack from Fifth Ward as well as from Sixth. However, the delivery of the thrust from the left is considerably simpler from Sixth Ward than from Fifth. Therefore it makes sense to learn the thrust from the left from Sixth Ward before learning it from Fifth Ward. Why Sixth Ward isn't simply named Fifth Ward is a mystery that will not be solved in this book.

The Sixth ward is not named in I.33. It is a low position used predominantly for thrusting, fulfilling the same function as the German ward *Pflug*, the ward of the *Plow*.[1] Hence the authors have chosen to use the name *Pflug*, despite some fairly obvious differences between the Sixth Ward and the normal *Pflug* of German Longsword.

Pflug is held with the left foot forward, with the buckler fully extended facing towards the opponent. The sword is pulled back with its point slightly to the right of the buckler, and the hand is in fourth position.[2] With a short enough sword the point might be hidden behind the buckler entirely, although this is not shown in I.33.

Figures 8.2 *The Sixth Ward:* Pflug, *"the plow."*

Pflug is countered by Half Shield. If the Priest adopts *Pflug*, and the Scholar responds with Half Shield, the Priest can immediately attack by passing forward and left, with the sword passing underneath the buckler arm and rising into the Student's face on the outside of his sword. The Priest's buckler provides opposition and prevents a parry by the Scholar.

Figures 8.2
A- The Priest in Pflug, *the Scholar in Half Shield.*
B- The Priest attacks with a thrust on a slope pace foward and left.

From Half Shield, the Scholar can respond to the thrust in the same way as he would to falling under the sword, by advancing with a bind and Shield-Knock

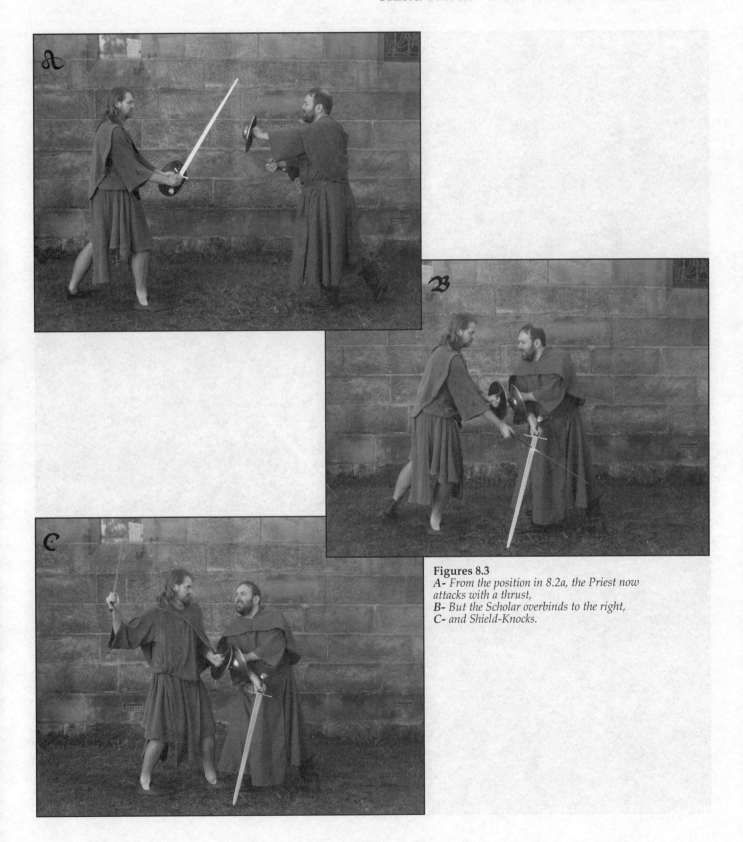

Figures 8.3
A- From the position in 8.2a, the Priest now attacks with a thrust,
B- But the Scholar overbinds to the right,
C- and Shield-Knocks.

If the Priest does not immediately attack, however, the Scholar can prevent the attack by binding the Priest's sword, specifically with an underbind on the left.[3] If the Priest still fails to respond, the Scholar can pass his buckler underneath his arm and deliver a Tread-Through, striking the Priest on the head.

Figures 8.4
A- The Priest in Pflug, the Scholar in Half Shield.
B- The Scholar underbinds on the left,
C- and then Treads-Through, opening a strike to
the head, or just about anyplace else.

Having been underbound, thus preventing the thrust, the Priest's only line of attack is to cut directly up at the Scholar's face. The Scholar can defend himself from this with a simple parry, again followed by a Thread-Through.

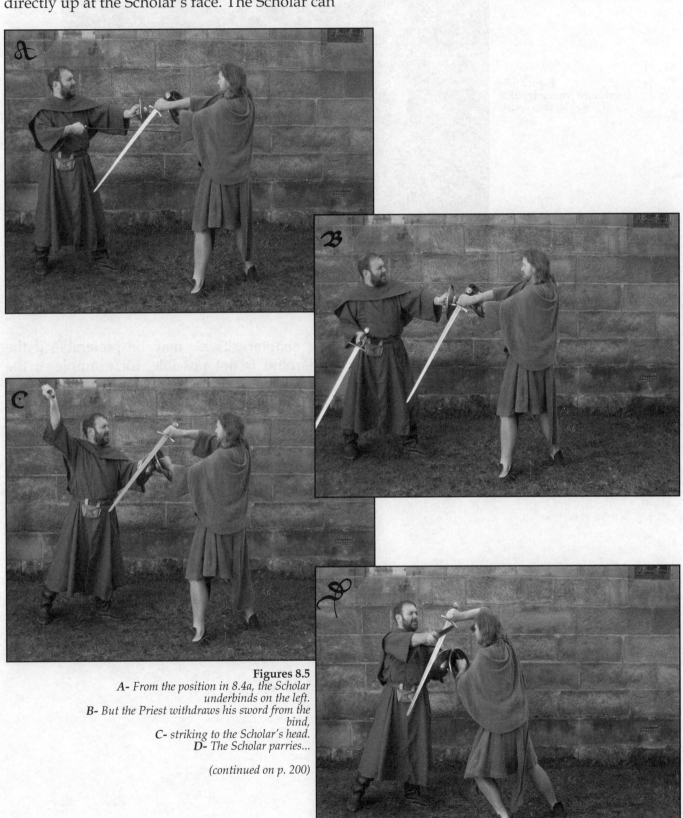

Figures 8.5
A- From the position in 8.4a, the Scholar underbinds on the left.
B- But the Priest withdraws his sword from the bind,
C- striking to the Scholar's head.
D- The Scholar parries...

(continued on p. 200)

Figure 8.5e
(continued from page 199)
E- ...and makes his own attack.

Half Shield is the only counter shown to *Pflug* as it allows the counterer to underbind the warder. However, other wards that allow the thrust from the left, such as *Nebenhut*, Tail Cover and the Priest's Special Longpoint, can also be used as counters (as will be demonstrated in the next chapter). These may be preferable if the underbind is not possible; for example, if the sword is fully withdrawn behind the buckler.

[1] Christian Tobler, *Secrets of German Medieval Swordsmanship*, Union City, 2001 p. 79

[2] Palm up, see Chapter 2

[3] I.33 does not describe the method by which the counterer should enter against *Pflug*. Given, however, the previous advice that from Half Shield you should "counterbind and step" (Plate 3), and that "the entire heart of the art of combat lies in…Longpoint" (Plate 2), the described sequence would seem an appropriate response from Half Shield, and is described in the Longpoint sequence on Plate 37 (lower) and 38.

CHAPTER 9
THE FIFTH WARD
"NEBENHUT"

The Fifth ward is not named in I.33. Similar wards are used in German and Italian medieval systems[1] and reflecting common usage in the historical fencing community the authors have dubbed the Fifth Ward *Nebenhut* or *Near* ward. It is held with the left leg forward, with the sword point directed back and to the left, hidden behind the body. The buckler is extended face-on at the opponent.

I.33 notes that from *Nebenhut* there are "two things to do. First, he can deliver a thrust; second, he can deliver a blow by dividing shield and sword." In other words, the warder can either deliver a thrust from the left on a pass forward and left, as seen from *Pflug*, or an *Oberhau* on a pass forward and right, using the buckler separately to clear a path for the attack. Both of these start with the same movement, an extension of the sword forwards and upwards towards the opponent's head, in many ways a mirror image of falling under the sword from the left.

Figure 9.1
The Nebenhut *from front and side.*

The First Counter ⸰ Half Shield

Nebenhut can be countered by Half Shield, although the author of I.33 notes that this can be risky, as "one must always beware of a blow being executed by the one standing in the guard, dividing the sword and shield with a blow."[2]

This means the Priest can start his rising blow, then simply use his sword and shield separately to bind Half Shield and strike the Scholar in the head or body.

Figures 9.2
A- The Priest in Nebenhut, *the Scholar in Half Shield.*
B- The Priest binds with his buckler,
C- and strikes the Scholar's head with an Oberhau.

Because of this danger, I.33 recommends that the Scholar "thrust without mercy" before the Priest can strike. This involves thrusting in such a way as to close off the Priest's only immediate line of attack, a technique similar to that used to counter Right Shoulder in Figure 5.14.

Figures 9.3
A- From the position in 9.2a, the Scholar "thrusts without mercy."
B- Note that the Scholar's thrust closes the Priest's line of attack.

The thrust from the left from *Nebenhut* is slightly more deceptive than from *Pflug*. The sword is swung forward and up, as if delivering a blow at the opponent's head. As with falling under the sword, the aim of the attack is to evoke the obvious response from the ordinary fencer, that of a reactive parry or attempted Stab-Knock. If the Scholar commits to his defence, or even if he fails to respond, the Priest sweeps the sword down in front of him and passes forward and left, using his buckler to close the line against the Scholar's sword while delivering a thrust into his face.

Figures 9.4
*A- The Priest adopts Nebenhut, the Scholar Half
Shield.*
B- Priest attacks with an Unterhau.
*C- The Scholar's attempted parry is deceived by
the Priest,*
D- who delivers a thrust from the left.

From Half Shield, the Scholar can respond to the thrust from the left in the same way as he would to falling under the sword, by advancing with a bind and Shield-Knock

Figures 9.4

A- Once again the Priest adopts Nebenhut *and the Scholar Half Shield.*
B- The Priest attacks with a thrust from the left.
C- This time the Scholar binds and Shield-Knocks,
D- and finishes with a cut.

However, because of the deceptive nature of the attack from *Nebenhut*, performing a Shield-Knock is not always possible. The initial extension cannot be entirely ignored, as seen in Fig. 9.2 above. Because of the time available to the attacker during his extension, the Stab-Knock used in Fig. 9.3 above is vulnerable to both deception and the thrust from the left. The alternative is to ward the initial *Unterhau* with a simple point down parry in a similar position to the Crutch. If this is successful, then the Scholar can follow up with a Shield-Knock.

Figures 9.6
A- From the position in 9.4a, the Priest attacks with an Unterhau,
B- before this can change into a thrust from the left, the Scholar parries with Crutch,
C- binding the Priest's buckler and cutting to the head.

If this parry is deceived by the thrust from the left, it is relatively simple to bring the sword back to the right to set aside the thrust. Normally, point-down parries are not recommended as they leave the defender underbound, and vulnerable to a Tread-Through (see Fig. 4.7). In this case, however, the combination of characteristics of the attack (the time taken, the committal of body weight, the position of the attacker's hands, and the fact the attack is a thrust, not a blow) leave the defender with the initiative, and the ability to execute a parry and Shield-Knock.

Figures 9.7
A- The Priest in Nebenhut, *the Scholar in Half Shield.*
B- The Priest attacks with a thrust from the left, which the Scholar parries in Crutch.
C- The Scholar Shield-Knocks (note how the parry has caught the Priest off-balance, halfway through a pass),
D- and finishes with a thrust.

The Second Counter ⁃ Tail Cover

The second counter to *Nebenhut* is simply called "a rare and very good counter."[3] We will call this counter Tail Cover. It is held with the right leg forward, with the buckler facing towards the opponent. Unlike Half Shield or *Pflug*, where the sword is extended, giving the opponent the opportunity to bind it, the point of the sword is dropped low to lie across the inside of the right leg. The hand is held palm-up.

Figure 9.8 *Tail cover*

Tail Cover counters a direct attack to the leg. If the Priest attacks the leg in a forceful manner, the Scholar can parry by stepping to the left, into the blow, and striking immediately back at the Priest's leg. The leg cut may not disable the Priest, but should distract him long enough to do something more lethal.

Figures 9.9
A- The Priest in Nebenhut, the Scholar in Tail Cover.
B- The Priest initiates the attack with a leg cut and the Scholar steps left.
C- And parries,

D- *Returning the favor by cutting at the Priest's leg with the false edge,*
E- The Scholar withdraws his point,
F- and thrusts,
G- before passing forward and into the Priest, throwing him.

One of the secrets of Tail Cover's efficacy is that each of its defences is initiated by this step to the left with the right foot, the same footwork used when "falling under the sword." The attacker's initial extension from *Nebenhut* is always matched by a cross-step from the defender in Tail Cover; this robs the attacker of some of the time he has to redirect his blow, and allows the defender to dominate the potential line of attack.

If the Priest is delivering a blow "by dividing shield and sword," the Scholar can avoid being bound by the shield because his point is low, but he can raise his point to strike the incoming blow upward, deflecting it away to the right.

Figures 9.10
A- From the position in 9.9a, the Priest attacks with a separated sword and buckler. The Scholar steps left,
B- striking the blow away and to the right.
C- He cuts to the Priest's face with a slope pace forward and left,
D- or passes forward, binds and Shield-Knocks.

If the Priest attacks with a thrust from the left, the Scholar can perform his own thrust from the left. Tail Cover demonstrates a basic principle of defending against the thrust from the left; that the best defence is a thrust from the left of your own, and it is more effective from a right-leg-forward stance, performed on a pass forward and left.

Figures 9.11
A- The Priest in Nebenhut, *the Scholar counters with Tail Cover.*
B- The Priest attacks with a thrust from the left while the Scholar steps left,
C- and defends with a thrust from the left on a slope forward and left.

If the Priest attempts a blow or bind, aggressively pressing forwards, the same defence can be delivered on a step back and left. Even if the thrust is unsuccessful, the Scholar is able to deflect or parry the Priest's sword to the right as shown in Figure 9.10.

Figures 9.12
A- The Priest in Nebenhut, *the Scholar in Tail Cover.*
B- The Priest opens by attacking with a separated sword and buckler, which cues the Scholar to step left.
C- defending with a thrust from the left as he steps back and left.

Tail Cover can also perform the point-down parry seen in Fig. 9.6 above.

The last counter to Nebenhut is the Priest's Special Longpoint. This ward works in almost exactly the same way as Tail Cover, and will be explored in detail in Chapter 11.

Figures 9.13
A- From the position in 9.12a, the Priest attacks with a thrust from the left. This time the Scholar steps left and parries in Crutch.
B- The Scholar simply binds with his buckler and cuts to the head.

⸲ NOTES ⸲

[1] For example, Ringeck's *Nebenhut*, see Christian Tobler, *Secrets of German Medieval Swordsmanship*, Union City, 2001, p. 155 and Fiore Dei Liberi's *Posta di Coda longa distesa* ("position of the long stretched tail"), *Flos Duellatorum*, 1409, Carta 19A Fig. 158.

[2] Jeffrey L. Forgeng, ***The Art of Medieval Swordsmanship***: *A Facsimile & Translation of Europe's Oldest Personal Combat Treatise, Royal Armouries MS. I33*, Union City, 2003, Plate 55.
[3] Ibid. Plate 57.

CHAPTER 10
THE SEVENTH WARD "LONGPOINT"

To a certain extent this chapter recaps material from earlier chapters because, as the author of I.33 states, "the entire heart of the art of combat lies in this final guard, which is called Longpoint; and all actions of the guards or of the sword finish or have their conclusion in this one, and not in others. Therefore study it more than the aforementioned first guard."[1] As stated earlier in this book, this statement doesn't mean that Longpoint is the best ward, merely that it's the one you will be in at the end of each action where you extend your sword. As such, many of the actions performed from and against Longpoint have already been discussed. However, there are a number of techniques involving Longpoint that were not already discussed in the chapters on the other wards.

There are three forms of Longpoint, not counting the "Priest's Special Longpoint" which we will detail in Chapter 11. *Low Longpoint* is held with the point extended downwards at approximately forty-five degrees below horizontal, *Middle Longpoint* has the point extended horizontally at chest height, and *High Longpoint* is held with the point extended up at approximately thirty degrees above horizontal. The buckler is often held passed underneath the forearm to the right of the blade, which allows the sword arm to be rested on the shield arm, helping to maintain this otherwise tiring ward.

Figures 10.1
A- Low Longpoint.
B- Middle Longpoint.
C- High Longpoint.

COUNTERING LONGPOINT

Although the author of I.33 did not think much of Longpoint as a ward, it is also clear that it was adopted by "ordinary fencers," and thus he details a number of methods by which the ward can be defeated.

There are no covers to Longpoint. However, in the majority of cases discussed by the author of I.33 there is no need to form a cover or counter, as Longpoint has little offensive potential. Since Longpoint is formed with the blade extended, as if the first move of the fight has already been made, the Scholar can immediately bind the Priest's extended sword.

The first bind described is the classic overbind on the right, the bind that precedes the Shield-Knock. The only difference between this bind and the bind made when the Priest falls under the sword in Underarm (see Chapter 4) is that the Priest's blade is stationary when the Scholar's bind is made. This subtly changes the dynamic. The Priest, knowing that the Scholar intends to perform a Shield-Knock, will pass forward, raising his sword and buckler into a position approximating the Crutch to provide protection for the left side of his head. The Scholar should prevent this, by rapidly completing his Shield-Knock. If the Scholar fails to complete his Shield-Knock rapidly enough and his sword is blocked by the Priest's then he is in a very vulnerable position as the Priest is already binding his buckler, and the Scholar may be cut on the head.

Figure 10.2a
A- The Priest adopts Low Longpoint, the Scholar overbinds.

(continued next page)

Figures 10.2:
(Continued from p. 221)
B- *The Priest passes forward, raising his hand into the Crutch.*
C- *He binds with the buckler.*
D- *Alternatively, the Scholar beats him to the punch and Shield-Knocks.*
E- *Or the Scholar's attack is parried, from which position the Priest could cut to the Scholar's head.*

The overbind on the right is the most commonly used bind in I.33, so anyone being bound in this way will know what is in store for them. Therefore it is possible that if the Priest is bound in this way, he will attempt to flee. If the Priest attempts to withdraw his sword into the ward of Underarm, the Scholar should pursue him, striking him on the left side of the head, even if the Priest is too far away for the Scholar to Shield-Knock.

Figures 10.3
A- From the position in figure 10.2a, the Priest withdraws into Underarm.
B- The Scholar passes forward, binding with the buckler and striking him.

The next bind that is described is the underbind on the left. If the Priest adopts Low Longpoint, the Scholar underbinds on the left.[2] The Priest immediately disengages in a clockwise direction and thrusts in the outside line. As the author of I.33 writes, "When one underbinds, the head of the one who binds is hit."[3] The Scholar responds to the thrust by rotating his hands clockwise and parrying the thrust. He can then overbind the Priest to the right with his sword and perform a Shield-Knock.

Figures 10.4
A- The Priest adopts Low Longpoint, the Scholar underbinds.
B- The Priest thrusts to the Scholar's face,
C- but the Scholar parries,
D- binds and advances.

The third bind described is the overbind on the left. If the Priest is in Low Longpoint and the Scholar overbinds on the left then the Priest can do what he did above, disengage from the bind and thrust at the Scholar's face.

Figures 10.5
A- The Priest in Low Longpoint, the Scholar overbinds.
B- The Priest simply disengages and thrusts to the Scholar's face.

The fourth bind, the underbind on the right is not described, no doubt for a very good reason. We have chosen not to suggest a sequence of events that follow an underbind on the right, because it is probably a very silly thing to do.

There is an alternative to binding. If the Priest adopts Low Longpoint, the Scholar may simply step in with a thrust, creating opposition in the outside line and controlling the Priest's sword.

Figures 10.6
A- The Priest takes Low Longpoint,
B- but the Scholar advances
aggressively and thrusts.

HIGH LONGPOINT

High Longpoint has an advantage over Low Longpoint due to gravity. From the high position it is easier to overbind your opponent. We have seen above that by far the most effective bind is the overbind on the right. If the Priest adopts High Longpoint, the Scholar may attempt to overbind him on the right. However, as the Scholar's blade approaches the Priest's the latter can drop his sword, gaining leverage from gravity and thereby achieving his own overbind on the right. From this position everything follows as was described in Chapter 4.

Figures 10.7
A- The Priest takes High Longpoint.
B- The Scholar tries to overbind,
C- but the Priest drops his blade to the right,
gaining leverage,
D- and completing his own overbind.

FIDDLEBOW

In the section on Longpoint, the author of I.33 introduces an eighth ward called Fiddlebow. Fiddlebow is held left foot forward with the buckler extended in front of the body and somewhat to the right. The sword rests on the left arm. Fiddlebow looks like a lazy form of Half Shield, but leaves a tempting gap that an opponent may try to exploit.

Figure 10.8
Fiddlebow.

Fiddlebow is not a counter. Rather, its entire purpose is to draw an unwary opponent into adopting Middle Longpoint.[4] It does this by leaving an inviting gap through which a thrust can be launched. If the Priest adopts Fiddlebow, the Scholar adopts Middle Longpoint, immediately thrusting into the gap, towards the Priest's face. The Priest rotates his sword to the right and his buckler to the left, taking the Scholar's point off line and stopping its motion. The Priest immediately turns his left hand, grabs the Scholar's blade in his left hand and levers it out of the Scholar's hand. The Priest can then cut at the Scholar's face.

Figures 10.9
A- The Priest adopts Fiddlebow, the Scholar thrusts.
B, C, D- The Priest levers the Scholar's sword out of his hand. with a scissor action between the sword and shield,
E- and strikes the Scholar in the face.

If the Priest fails to grab the Scholar's sword in his left hand, he can still overbind the Scholar to the right, from which everything follows that has been described before.

Figures 10.10
A- The Priest adopts Fiddlebow, the Scholar thrusts.
B- The Priest tries to lever the Scholar's sword out of his hand, but fails,

Figures 10.10
(Continued from page 230)
C- and overbinds instead,
D- completing a Shield-Knock,
E- then cutting for the Scholar's head.

'⁓ NOTES ⁓'

[1] Jeffrey L. Forgeng, ***The Art of Medieval Swordsmanship***: *A Facsimile and Translation of Europe's Oldest Personal Combat Treatise, Royal Armouries MS. I.33*, Union City, 2003, Plate 2.
[2] Underbinding can be a little confusing. In an underbind on the right the point of the sword faces to the left and the bind moves clockwise. In an underbind on the left, the point faces right and the bind moves counterclockwise.

[3] Forgeng, 2003, Plate 38
[4] If Middle Longpoint has already been adopted, there would seem no reason why the counterer could not respond with Fiddlebow.

Chapter 11
Priest's Special Longpoint

In the last few chapters we have referred regularly to a ward called the Priest's Special Longpoint, although we have avoided discussing it closely. The reason is that almost the entire I.33 system of sword and buckler can be performed from this single ward. The Priest's Special Longpoint mimics elements of nearly all of the useful wards, covers and counters in the rest of the manuscript, and is in effect the only ward you really need to know. Having explored all of the other wards, and the principles they illustrate, we can now use the Priest's Special Longpoint as a one-ward summary of the entire system.

The Priest's Special Longpoint is probably the most controversial position in the manuscript. It has been called "physically implausible,"[1] and indeed it certainly illustrates the limitations of I.33's artwork. The ward is held with the right foot forward, with the sword pointing down and backwards on the left hand side of the body (as in Underarm), but with the hand in First position i.e. with knuckles upwards.[2] The buckler is held back and withdrawn, so as not to impede the sword's movement. The Priest's Special Longpoint does not appear to have any attributes in common with any other variety of Longpoint in the manuscript, except that it can readily be converted into Longpoint by simply extending the arm and flipping the point forward.

From Priest's Special Longpoint you can fall under the sword as easily as you can from Underarm, but without the danger of being bound as seen in Fig. 3.28. The ward can also perform a thrust from the left as easily as from *Pflug*, and acts as a substitute for both the Crutch and Half Shield, as well as countering all other wards.

Figures 11.1

A- Priest and Scholar in the Priest's Special Longpoint.
B- Extension into Middle Longpoint.

COUNTERING OTHER WARDS

The Priest's Special Longpoint is used as a counter to a number of wards in I.33, and would appear to be capable of countering every other ward.

Against the Priest in Right Shoulder, the Scholar can protect himself from sudden attack in the same way as seen from Underarm in Figures 4.2 and 4.3.

Figures 11.2
A- *The Priest in Right Shoulder, the Scholar adopts the Priest's Special Longpoint.*
B- *The Priest delivers a Oberhau on a pass forward and right while the Scholar falls under his sword.*
C- *The Scholar binds with the buckler and thrusts to the Priest's head.*
D- *Alternatively, as the Priest delivers his Oberhau, the Scholar lifts his sword to parry the blow while stepping forward and left.*
E- *The Scholar now binds with the buckler and ripostes to the Priest's head.*

The Scholar can also offend the Priest by simply passing forward with a thrust between the Priest's sword and shield, as in Fig. 5.14.

Figures 11.3
*A- The Priest once again begins in Right Shoulder, while the Scholar counters with the Priest's Special Longpoint.
B- Since the Priest does not initiate an attack, the Scholar enters quickly with a thrust.*

Countering the Priest in Left Shoulder, the Scholar in Priest's Special Longpoint can immediately attack with a thrust from the left, or respond to a left *Oberhau* in the same manner.

Figures 11.4
A- The Priest now takes Left Shoulder, while the Scholar takes Priest's Special Longpoint.
B- The Scholar enters with a thrust.
C- Alternatively, the Priest attacks, but the Scholar again replies with a thrust.

If the Priest adopts *vom Tag*, the Scholar in Priest's Special Longpoint can defend himself from any attack as in 11.2 above, or can immediately enter with High Cover, as seen in Fig. 7.2.

Figures 11.5
A- *The Priest in vom Tag, the Scholar in Priest's Special Longpoint.*
B- *The Scholar executes a High Cover*
C- *and strikes at the Priest's sword arm,*
D- *causing the Priest to retreat. The Scholar then thrusts into the Priest's breast.*
E- *Alternatively, the Priest strikes, and the Scholar parries,*
F- *binding with the buckler and riposting to the Priest's head.*

If the Priest adopts *Pflug*, the Scholar can attack with a thrust from the left, or wait for the Priest to attack, and respond in the same manner.

Figures 11.6
A- The Priest tries Pflug, *against the Scholar in Priest's Special Longpoint.*
B- The Scholar enters with a thrust to the left,
C- or the Priest attacks with a thrust from the left,
D- and the Scholar defends with his own thrust from the left.

Against *Nebenhut*, the Scholar in Priest's Special Longpoint has all the options available from either Half Shield or Tail Cover shown in Chapter 9. If the Priest does not attack, he can enter with the thrust, as seen above.

Figures 11.7

A- The Priest in Nebenhut, *the Scholar in Priest's Special Longpoint.*
B- The Scholar moves in aggressively from the left with a thrust.

If the Priest in *Nebenhut* attacks with a thrust from the left, the Scholar can respond with either his own thrust, an overbind on the right and Shield-Knock, or an underbind on the left (a point-down parry) and Shield-Knock

Figures 11.8
A- From the position in 11.7a, the Priest attacks with a thrust from the left.
B- The Scholar defends himself, also using a thrust from the left.
C- Or he binds right,
D- and Shield-Knocks.
E- Or he parries with a Crutch,
F- and Shield-Knocks.

If the Priest attacks with his sword and shield separated, the Scholar steps back and left and responds with either his own cut or thrust, or a parry followed by a thrust or Shield-Knock

Figures 11.9
A-The Priest in Nebenhut *and the Scholar in Priest's Special Longpoint.*
B- The Priest attacks with his sword and buckler separated.
C- The Scholar defends using a thrust from the left on a step left and back.
D- Or parries the attack aside,
E- and thrusts,
F- or passes forward with a Shield-Knock.

Against the Priest lying in any of the other forms of Longpoint, the Scholar can immediately bind in any of the ways shown in Chapter 10.

Finally, against the Priest in Underarm the Scholar in Priest's Special Longpoint has all the many and varied options available from either Half Shield or the Crutch outlined in Chapter 4.

Figures 11.10
A- *The Priest in Middle Longpoint, the Scholar in Priest's Special Longpoint.*
B- *The Scholar overbinds on the right,*
C- *and Treads-Through.*

THE FIRST COUNTER ⁄ HALF SHIELD

Having been countered by the Priest's Special Longpoint, the Priest will not want to remain in his ward. Instead he will adopt a counter.

The Priest's Special Longpoint can first be countered by Half Shield. The Scholar can respond to this is a number of way. The first is to execute a thrust from the left, and a second option is to fall under the sword. The Priest can defend himself with a Shield-Knock, as seen many times previously (e.g. Fig. 8.3). The Scholar, however, has one more trick up his sleeve.

If the Scholar falls under the sword and is bound by the Priest, he can simply cede the bind and wind his sword and buckler into High Cover. This will cause the Priest's sword to slide harmlessly off his blade, allowing the Scholar to Tread Through with a Shield-Knock. This is a variation of play unique to the Priest's Special Longpoint.

The reason this is possible from Priest's Special Longpoint and not from Underarm is due to subtle difference in the angle of attack when falling under the sword. Remember in Chapter 4 we noted that when overbinding the attack from Underarm it was vital to perform this edge-to-edge and *störck* to *störck* to prevent the attacker from powering through the defence. This case is different. The same attack from Priest's Special Longpoint has a more vertical trajectory than from Underarm, and as a result the attacker presents the flat of their blade to the defender. When the bind is made, the attacker has no strength at all to withstand the fairly vigorous bind, and thus the defender's blade will power straight through the attack without binding it. The inherent weakness of the flat of the sword frees the attacker's blade and allows the Tread-Through.

Figures 11.11
A- *The Scholar is in Priest's Special Longpoint, the Priest in Half Shield.*
B- *The Scholar falls under the sword,*
C- *while the Priest binds,*
D- *and the Scholar is forced to cede to High Cover,*
E- *but Treads-Through.*

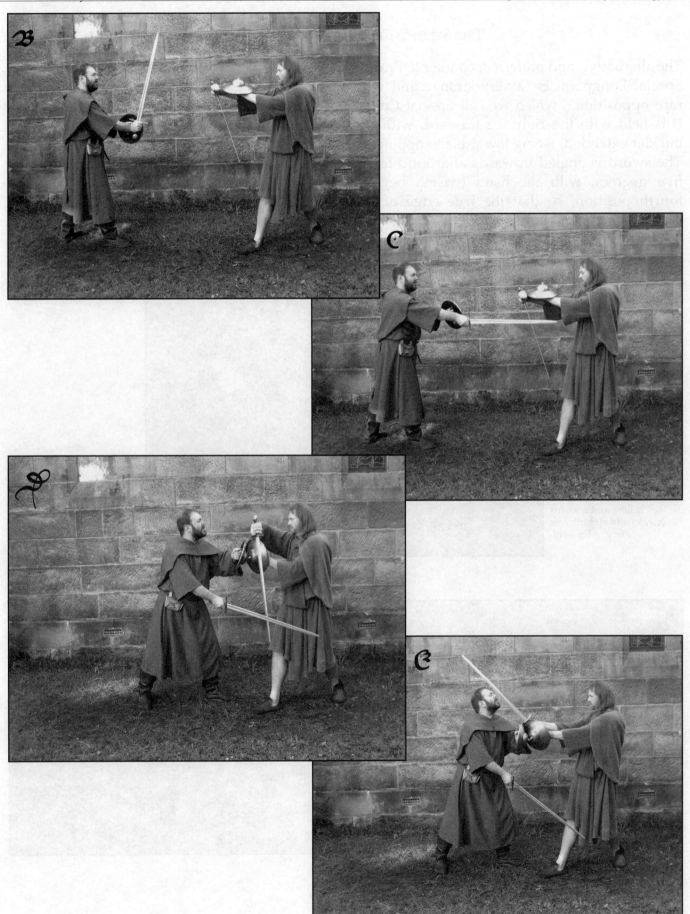

THE SECOND COUNTER · SPECIAL COVER

The alternative, and preferred, counter to Priest's Special Longpoint is "a very strange and very rare opposition"[3] which we call Special Cover. It is held with the right leg forward, with the buckler extended, facing towards the opponent. The sword is angled upwards at around forty-five degrees, with the hand twisted beyond fourth position, so that the true edge of the sword is facing upwards.

Special Cover counters the Priest's Special Longpoint in exactly the same way Half Shield counters Underarm. If the Scholar fails to attack, the Priest can pass forward, binding the Scholar's sword arm with his buckler, and deliver a powerful reverse stroke to the Scholar's head.

Figures 11.13:
A- Special Cover from the front and side.
B- The Scholar in Priest's Special Longpoint, the Priest in Special Cover.
C- The Priest passes forward, binding the Scholar's arm with his buckler and striking him firmly in the head.

If the Scholar falls under the sword, the play is exactly as seen from Half Shield and Underarm. If the Scholar falls under the sword, the position of the sword in Special Cover allows the Priest to strike the edge of the Scholar's sword with a more powerful outward beat than available from Half Shield, preventing the Scholar from Treading Through, and producing the familiar Shield-Knock.

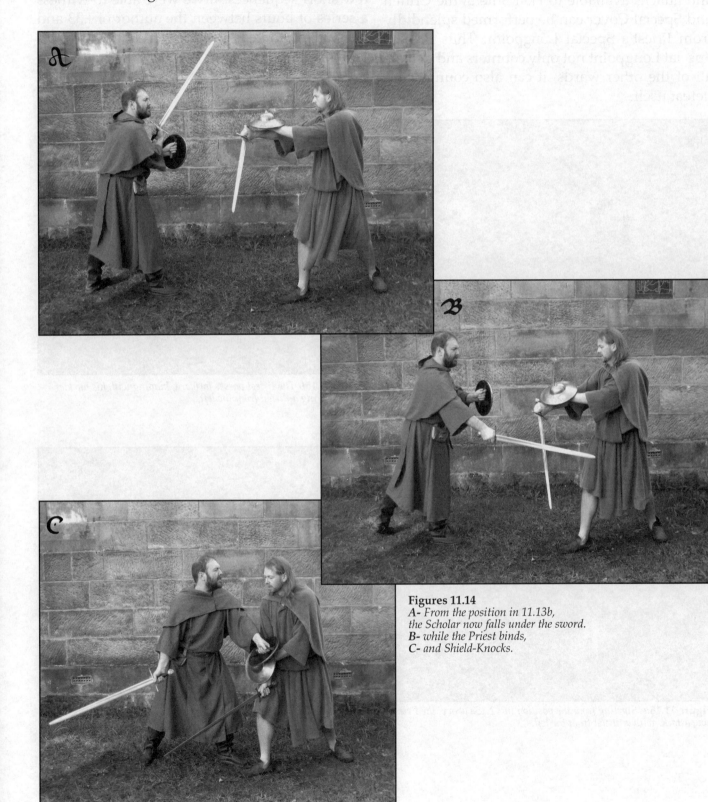

Figures 11.14
A- From the position in 11.13b,
the Scholar now falls under the sword.
B- while the Priest binds,
C- and Shield-Knocks.

THE THIRD COUNTER - PRIEST'S SPECIAL LONGPOINT ITSELF

Just as Underarm may counter itself, so may Priest's Special Longpoint. All of the defences and attacks available to Half Shield, the Crutch and Special Cover can be performed splendidly from Priest's Special Longpoint. Thus Priest's Special Longpoint not only counters and defeats all of the other wards, it can also counter and defeat itself.

In essence, the entire I.33 method of sword and buckler can be distilled into this one ward and a few short sequences. If we were able to witness a series of bouts between the author of I.33 and his student, there is a very good chance it would look like this.

Figure 11.15a *Priest and Scholar both adopt Priest's Special Longpoint.*

Figure 11.15b *The Priest passes forward, binding with his buckler and delivering a thrust from the left.*

Figure 11.16a *Starting from the position in 11.15a above, the Priest now attacks with a thrust from the left.*

Figure 11.16b *But the Scholar counters with a thrust from the left of his own.*

Figure 11.17a *Starting from the position in 11.15a, the Priest falls under the sword.*

Figure 11.17b
This time the Scholar binds and Shield-Knocks.

Figure 11.18a *Starting from the position in 11.17a (above), the Scholar slope paces forward and left into the Crutch, parries...*

Figure 11.18b
...and grapples.

✎ NOTES ✎

[1] Jeffrey L. Forgeng, ***The Art of Medieval Swordsmanship***: *A Facsimile and Translation of Europe's Oldest Personal Combat Treatise, Royal Armouries MS. I.33*, Union City, 2003, p. 7.

[2] In the manuscript this is indicated by the fact that the warder's wrist is below the line of the sword.

[3] Forgeng, 2003, Plate 49.

CHAPTER 12
WALPURGIS' WARD

The very last ward in I.33 is the "Priest's special second ward", held by a female character called Walpurgis.[1] The presence of this female combatant in I.33 might present practical self-defence for sisters of the Church, or indicate I.33 was intended as training for judicial duels, in which females were also expected to participate. More likely though is that this is I.33's variant of a favourite medieval theme, the guard of the woman[2] in which an illusion of fear or weakness is given to draw the opponent into a rash action. The fencer in Walpurgis' ward is holding back, almost cowering away from her attacker. Of course this is an illusion. Adopting this ward, you want to appear weak and defenceless, but of course you are not.

Walpurgis' Ward is adopted as a counter to Underarm, but is one of the few positions in which you can safely lie for any length of time. It is held with the sword vertical, in front of the right shoulder, where it cannot be bound. The sword can be held here for a long time without muscle strain. The buckler, too, is held tucked into the body, facing to the right, inviting an attack to the left shoulder. The left leg is forward.

Figure 12.1
Walpurgis in her ward.

251

Walpurgis' Ward is a very secure defensive stance against most forms of attack, even though it appears as if the warder is cowering from their opponent. If the Priest attacks the obvious opening, from say Right Shoulder, Walpurgis need only pass forward and right to achieve a Stab-Knock.

Figures 12.2
A- Walpurgis in her ward, the Priest adopts Right Shoulder.
B- The Priest initiates the attack with an Oberhau.
C- Walpurgis passes forward and right with a Stab-Knock.

Any attempt to bind the tucked-in buckler will also fail, as Walpurgis' sword will remain free and able to attack the binding arm.

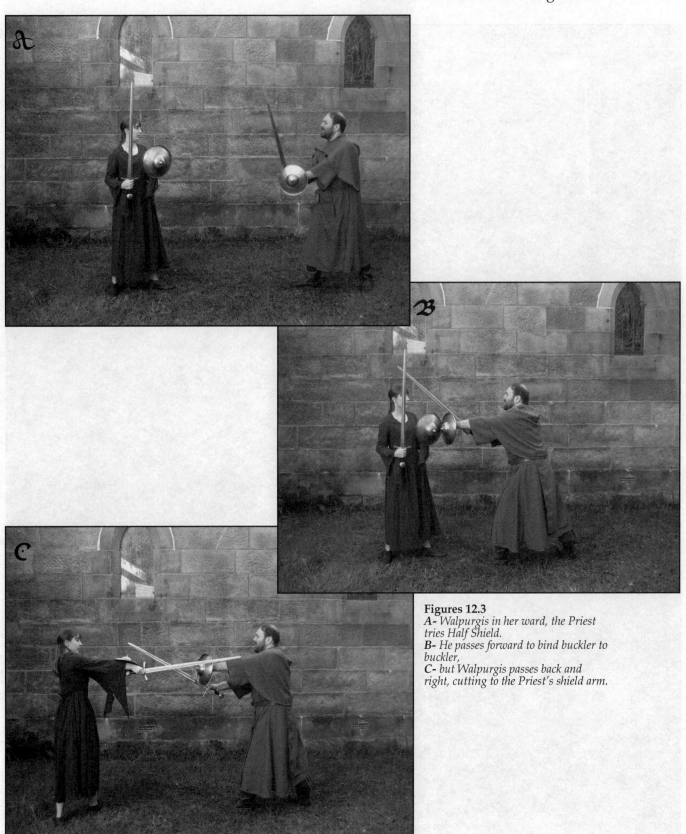

Figures 12.3
A- Walpurgis in her ward, the Priest tries Half Shield.
B- He passes forward to bind buckler to buckler,
C- but Walpurgis passes back and right, cutting to the Priest's shield arm.

I.33 shows Walpurgis' Ward as a counter to Underarm, but even here it is relatively secure. If the Priest falls under the sword, he swings his sword directly into Walpurgis' buckler, allowing her to respond with a Stab-Knock.

Figures 12.4:
A- Walpurgis in her Ward, the Priest in Underarm.
B- The Priest falls under the sword,
C- Walpurgis passes forward and right with a Stab-Knock.

If the Priest is in Underarm and fails to fall under the sword, Walpurgis may pass forward rapidly into Half Shield and then again to bind the Priest's sword and buckler, which, as the author of I.33 points out, "will be very detrimental to the one standing in the guard."[3]

Figures 12.5
A- Walpurgis keeps her ward, and the Priest once more tries Underarm.
B- Walpurgis passes forward into Half Shield,
C- and continues to pass forward again into a bind.

The response of the Priest is to make a small step to the right and adopt High Cover, the same counter we saw in Chapter 7, where it countered *vom Tag*. In that case High Cover was used to deliver a rising cut to the warder's arm or a thrust from the left to their face; Walpurgis however, is proof against either of these attacks. High Cover does close the line against any direct attack by Walpurgis, and if she fails to react, gives the Priest an opportunity to cut upwards at her buckler-arm.

Figures 12.6
*A- Walpurgis keeps her ward, while the
Priest adopts Underarm.
B- The Priest now passes forward into
High Cover,
C- and passes forward with an
Unterhau to Walpurgis' arm.*

Walpurgis' reaction to this Cover is to drop the sword and buckler down and overbind to the right. This prevents the *Unterhau*, and gives Walpurgis the opportunity to perform a Shield-Knock. While the bind and Shield-Knock as performed from Half Shield against Underarm must be performed strongly and vigorously, Walpurgis does not push her attack with the same power. If she binds too strongly, the Priest's blade will slide out of the bind and allow him to parry any attack, or even strike her. Her Shield-Knock is done quickly on a short lunge, her buckler simply holding the Priest's weapons in place, rather than binding them strongly to his body.

Figure 12.7a: *From the previous start and after the Priest has stepped into High Cover, Walpurgis now overbinds the Priest's sword.*

Figure 12.7b: *She Shield-Knocks on a short lunge...*

Figure 12.7c: *...and hopefully strikes some sense into the Priest!*

[1] Saint Walpurgis was an 8th century English missionary who went to Germany to assist St. Boniface and became abbess of Heidenheim. She is best remembered for having lent her name to *Walpurgisnacht*, the traditional German witches' sabbath and "Satan's Birthday," when, in medieval and Renaissance times witches assembled on the Harz mountain tops to consort with the Devil, as featured in the famous scene in Goethe's *Faust*. Why St Walpurgis' name became attached to the witches' sabbath is unknown - perhaps simply because it coincidently occurs on the eve of her feast day, May 1st - but this is not even her primary feast day, only a translation feast acknowledging when some of her bones were moved. It could be that, as the church tried to bend *Walpurgisnacht* into a festival to drive out evil spirits with noise and bonfires, St Walpurgis, who was known as a protectoress against witchcraft and sorcery, was deliberately celebrated. A final suggestion is that there was an old fertility goddess named Waldborg in the region where St Walpurgis set up her monastery, and the names became confused over time.

[2] Early medieval Italian masters included a similar position they named the *posta di donna*, or "Woman's Stance." In his *Fior di Battaglia* of 1409 (Getty MS 83MR183), Fiore dei Liberi has three different variants of his "posta di donna": *I am called the guardia and the posta di donna because among these other prese of the sword it is like a woman, for one does not have this presa but another* (Carta 24V) and, *This also is posta di donna la soprana that with her wiles she often beguiles the other guards.* (Carta 24V). Translation by Bob Charron. Seven decades later, Fillipo Vadi also included a slightly different variant of the stance, which was nearly identical to our Walpurgis' Ward: *I am the woman's stance and I am not without use, because the sword's length often deceives.* Translated by Luca Porzio in *Arte Gladiatoria Dimicandi: 15th Century Swordsmanship of Filippo Vadi*, Union City, 2003.

[3] Jeffrey L. Forgeng, ***The Art of Medieval Swordsmanship***: *A Facsimile and Translation of Europe's Oldest Personal Combat Treatise, Royal Armouries MS. I.33,* Union City, 2003, Plate 63.

CHAPTER 13
CONCLUSIONS

One of the first questions that many of you will be asking yourselves is "where do we go now?" This is a good question. This book is not set down as individual lessons, but rather, follows the organization of the original manuscript. I.33 is laid out extremely systematically. In fact it is so close to a lesson plan that we didn't want to change it. The fundamental principles of the style are all contained in the first four pages of the manuscript. From there each ward, its counters, how to bind and enter against the counter etc., are presented systematically. You could do a lot worse than to work through each technique shown in the book in turn. However, as the authors have been learning and teaching I.33, let us present a brief lesson plan based on what has been presented in the preceding chapters.

Lesson 1. Footwork: We have yet to see a good fencer with poor footwork. Practice all of the different movements listed in Chapter 2.

Lesson 2. Ward and Counter: We have included below a list of wards and counters. You should practice the opening stage of a fight, where one fencer adopts a ward while entering wide distance and the other immediately adopts a counter. Start by adopting known wards and counters, but move up to a drill where either fencer may initiate the action by adopting a ward and his drill partner must immediately form an appropriate counter.

Ward	Counter
Underarm	- Half Shield
	- Crutch
	- Extended Longpoint
	- Walpurgis
	- Underarm
	- Priest's Special Longpoint
Right Shoulder	- Right Cover
	- Half Shield
	- Priest's Special Longpoint
Left Shoulder	- Left Cover
	- Half Shield
	- Extended Longpoint
	- Priest's Special Longpoint
vom Tag	- Half Shield
	- Underarm
	- Priest's Special Longpoint
Pflug	- Half Shield
	- High Longpoint
Nebenhut	- Half Shield
	- Tail Cover
	- Priest's Special Longpoint
Longpoint	- No counters (you should immediately Bind)
Priest's Special Longpoint	- Half Shield
	- Special Cover

Lesson 3. Attacking and defending the Arm: The attacker should first discard his buckler. Then using the wards and counters above, he should make a range of attacks. The defender should parry the attack with the buckler and cut at the arm. The attacker should then make the same attacks with his buckler covering his arm. The defender should try to cut at the arm. This

should show how small a gap a sword can cut through and should help the attacker get used to covering the arm.

Lesson 4. Stab-Knocks:
Go through the range of Stab-Knocks in Chapter 3. There are additional Stab-Knocks in various chapters, but the ones in Chapter 3 should be sufficient to familiarise you with the concept.

Lesson 5. Falling Under the Sword and the Shield-Knock:
With the attacker in Underarm and the Defender in Half Shield the attacker should fall under the sword (as described in Chapter 3). The Counterer should first try to defend himself incorrectly, by a simple parry, a Stab-Knock and by cutting down at the attacker's head. The attacker should complete his attack against each defence as described in Chapter 3. The defender should then defend himself correctly by binding with the sword, advancing and performing a Shield-Knock as shown in Chapter 3.

Lesson 6. Responses to the Shield-Knock:
With the attacker in Underarm and the defender in Half Shield, the attacker should fall under the sword. The defender should perform a Shield-Knock as in the lesson above. The attacker should then respond to the Shield-Knock by a Tread Through, Change of Sword, Grapple or by Fleeing Sideways, all described in Chapter 4. Finally the attacker should make no attack, allowing the defender to attack him as described in Chapter 4.

Lesson 7. The Crutch:
Go through the sequences in the section on the Crutch in Chapter 4.

Lesson 8. Underarm vs. Extended Longpoint:
Go through the sequences in the section on Extended Longpoint in Chapter 4.

Lesson 9. Right Shoulder:
Go through the sequences in Chapter 5.

Lesson 10. Left Shoulder:
Go through the sequences in Chapter 6.

Lesson 11. *vom Tag*:
Go through the sequences in Chapter 7.

Lesson 12. *Pflug*:
Go through the sequences in Chapter 8.

Lesson 13. *Nebenhut*:
Go through the sequences in Chapter 9.

Lesson 14. Longpoint:
Go through the sequences in Chapter 10.

Lesson 15. Priest's Special Longpoint:
Go through the sequences in Chapter 11.

Lesson 16. Walpurgis' Ward:
Go through the sequences in Chapter 12.

Of course each lesson can be split over multiple sessions to focus on particular aspects that are troubling. After doing set drills, you can start to incorporate drills which involve choices. For instance you may create a drill where the attacker adopts Underarm. The defender must adopt Half Shield, the Crutch, Extended Longpoint or Walpurgis' Ward. The attacker must respond to the counter with an appropriate offensive action, falling under the sword etc. Or you may create a drill where the attacker in Underarm falls under the sword. The defender responds with a simple parry, a cut to the head or he may bind and Shield-Knock. The attacker must respond appropriately and hit the defender, in these cases respectively with a cut under the sword, a Stab-Knock or with a Tread Through/ Change of Sword, Grapple or Fleeing Sideways (see Chapter 4). The number of possible drills is endless, but their purpose is identical, to bridge the gap between a set drill, designed to train a response and reinforce muscle memory and actual free fencing in which the number of variables is often so great that people get hopelessly muddled.

The important thing to remember in any physical learning process is that you must first train your body to perform a movement and then practice that movement under increasing pressure until your body can do it at will, and often without any exercise of will. Fencing teachers for centuries have stressed the importance of not actually free fencing until that free fencing will be reinforcing a desired movement pattern. The quickest way to teach yourself bad habits is to do them in a bout with an opponent. Remember that replacing a faulty muscle memory takes approximately ten times the number of repetitions as it takes to implant the correct muscle memory first time.

Once you are confident that you have trained your body to move in a way that matches the I.33 system, you can profitably fence. There are two different ways of fencing competitively, both of which are useful. Firstly, you can fence with an opponent, without keeping score, or even particularly worrying about who was hit. This is called an assault. If you are trying to make a particular attack or defence work, then you should use it without fear of the consequences, repeating the action as many times as you need to, to get it right under pressure. Fencing in this manner is to test yourself and to hone your own skills against an uncooperative opponent. Often the most profitable assaults are those in which you are hit the most. If you never assault then you will reinforce those aspects of your style that are strong and neglect those that are weak. The only way to strengthen a weak area is to train it, and if you're worried about who's scoring hits then you will tend to use only those techniques that you already know you're good at.

The second way to fence is bouting, where you are trying to use your best technique to strike your opponent and avoid being struck, with or without counting hits. This is as important as any other part of training and after the initial skills have been mastered, it is imperative that you do regular bouting. Bouting not only tests your ability to perform the actions described in I.33, it develops the correct sense of timing and distance. Do not be in too much of a hurry to bout, but don't be frightened to start bouting when it's time. Every aspect of training is required to create a good fencer. However, as with anything in fencing, don't let defeat disturb you and don't let victory make you complacent. Treat every bout as a learning experience and try to take something positive out of it (even if that's knowing what you have to do more work on). Do not be frightened to take a step back from bouting to concentrate on drills and the occasional assault. Try to be constantly critical of your own performance, but don't become depressed by apparent failure to progress. Fencing literature is full of Masters saying that they've studied fencing all of their lives and have barely scratched the surface. If the greats say this, then we mere mortals should have no illusions about how rapid our progress is likely to be. Like all martial arts, swordsmanship is a lifelong journey and is as much about development of character and facing challenges as it is about becoming a living engine of destruction. Historical fencing is one of the least likely of all martial arts to ever be used in a practical situation. Therefore, we should explore these martial arts because of our interest in them. Anyone who expects to be mugged by someone with a sword and buckler on the way to training is in need of assistance not to be found in this book.

When approaching bouting, it is also worth remembering that many of the Priest's lessons are not necessarily intended to teach the Scholar the exact manner in which to fight, but to demonstrate important principles upon which the sword and buckler fight is founded; the use of Longpoint to illustrate various forms of binds is an obvious example. While I.33's system of wards and counters, binds and engagements may seem rather complicated and difficult to master, it is not necessary to remember every technique in the manuscript in order to defend yourself, merely to understand the underlying concepts, and the inherent weaknesses of various positions. The authors have found that, the more experienced they become in the I.33 system, the more they rely upon a single ward, the Priest's Special Longpoint, because as the author of I.33 himself said "know that all of these are reduced to the first ward and to the counter which is called Half Shield."[1]

Of course, as mentioned in Chapter 2, this book is best used in training under a competent instructor. Appendix A looks at how you might go about finding an instructor. If you are new to western swordsmanship and want to train using this book as a basis, please read and re-read the sections in Chapter 2 on what to wear and especially on the importance of control. Swords were designed to kill and must be respected as such. No armour is proof against everything. Even a wooden waster or a padded sword of correct weight can inflict serious injury, so treat your training partner as if he were yourself. We cannot make you act responsibly with a sword or a waster. Only one person can be responsible for your actions and that's you.

I.33 is the oldest fencing treatise currently known. It is also perhaps the best qualified of all the medieval treatises to refute Egerton Castle's unfortunate reference to "the rough untutored

fighting of the Middle Ages."[2] We defy anyone familiar with fencing to read this book and deny the skill and sophistication of medieval fencing. I.33 shows that medieval fencers had a sophisticated understanding of timing, distance and line, three of the fundamentals of all fencing, and were just as capable of performing complex fencing phrases comprised of multiple actions as are modern fencers. This should not really surprise anyone. People from all times and from all parts of the globe have shown the same capacity for problem solving. Give people an important enough problem, for example, "how do I keep the other chap from killing me with this sword?" and they will exercise all of their human ingenuity to solving that problem in the most efficient manner possible. People are not stupid.

I.33 shows us a glimpse of a complex system of fencing, at once brutal and beautiful in its efficiency. This is of course its appeal. In an age where mainstream fencing has irrevocably become a sport, many people are searching for something a little more martial. We hope that with our help, some of you have found what you're looking for in I.33.

' NOTES '

[1] Jeffrey L. Forgeng, *The Art of Medieval Swordsmanship*: A Facsimile and Translation of Europe's Oldest Personal Combat Treatise, Royal Armouries MS. I.33, Union City, 2003, Plate 49.

[2] Egerton Castle, Schools and Masters of the Fence from the Middle Ages to the Eighteenth Century. London 1885 p. 5

Allanson-Winn and Phillipps-Wolley, *Broadsword and Singlestick with chapters on Quarterstaff, Bayonet, Shillalah, Walking-Stick, Umbrella and Other Weapons of Self Defence*, London, 1890.

Capo Ferro, Ridolfo. *Gran Simulacro Dell'Arte Edell'Uso Della Scherma*, Siena, 1610.

Castle, Egerton. *Schools and Masters of the Fence from the Middle Ages to the Eighteenth Century*. London, 1885.

Dall'Agocchie, Giovanni. *Dell'Arte Discrimia Libri Tre*, Venetia, 1572.

Dei Liberi, Fiore. *Fior di Battaglia*, Italy, 1409 (MS Ludwig XV.13, Getty Museum, Los Angeles).

Die Manessesche Liederhandschrift, c. 1315.

di Grassi, Giacomo. *Ragione Di Adoprar Sicuramente L'Arme Si Da Offesa, Come Da Difesa*. Venetia, 1570.

di Grassi, Giacomo. *Di Grassi his true Arte of Defence*, London, 1594.

Fabris, Salvator. *De Lo Schermo Overo Scienza D'Arme*, Copenhagen, 1606.

Forgeng, Jeffrey L. **The Art of Medieval Swordsmanship**: *A Facsimile and Translation of Europe's Oldest Personal Combat Treatise, Royal Armouries MS. I.33*, Union City, 2003.

Gaugler, William M. *The History of Fencing: Foundations of Modern European Swordplay*, Bangor, Maine, 1998.

Giganti, Niccolo *Teatro*, Venetia, 1606.

Godfrey, John. *A Treatise Upon the Useful Science of Defence*, London, 1747,

Hand, Stephen. "Counterattacks with opposition: The influence of weapon form" in Stephen Hand (ed.) *SPADA*, Union City, 2003.

Hand, Stephen and Wagner, Paul. "Talhoffer's Sword and Duelling Shield Techniques as a Model for Reconstructing Early Medieval Sword and Shield Techniques," in Stephen Hand (editor) *SPADA*, Union City, 2003.

MacBane, Donald *The Expert Swordsman's Companion*, 1728, in Mark Rector (ed.), *Highland Swordsmanship*, Union City, 2001.

Macgregor, Archibald, *Macgregor's Lecture on the Art of Defence*, 1791.

Mele, Greg. "Much Ado About Nothing or The cutting Edge of Flat Parries" in Stephen Hand (ed.) *SPADA*, 2002.

Oakeshott, R.E. *The Sword in the Age of Chivalry*, London, 1964.

Porzio, Luca and Mele, Greg. *Arte Gladiatoria Dimicandi 15th Century Swordsmanship of Filippo Vadi*, Union City, 2003.

Silver, George. *Paradoxes of Defence*, London, 1599.

Silver, George. *Bref Instructions Upon My Paradoxes of Defence*, Sloane Manuscript 376, British Library, London, c. 1605.

Singman, Jeffrey L. "The Medieval Swordsman: a 13th-century German Fencing Manuscript" in, *Royal Armouries Yearbook Volume 2*, Royal Armouries Museum, Leeds, 1997.

Stowe, John. *The Annales; augmented unto the ende of this present yeere 1614 by Edmund Howes, Gent*, London, 1615.

Taylor, John. *The Art of Defence on Foot with the Broad Sword and Sabre: adapted also to the Spadroon, or Cut-and-Thrust Sword*, London, 1804.

Tobler, Christian. **Secrets of German Medieval Swordsmanship**: *Sigmund Ringeck's Commentaries on Johannes Liectenauer's Verse*, Union City, 2001.

Viggiani, Angelo. *Lo Schermo*, Vinetia, 1575.

Wagner, Paul. *Master of Defence: The Works of George Silver* Boulder, 2003.

Wilhalm, Jörg, *Fechtbüch*, c. 1520.

Zabinski, Grzegorz and Bartlomiei Walczak, *Codex Wallerstein*, Boulder, 2002.

Finding Instruction in Historical Fencing

It has been said that you can't learn a martial art from a book. We happen to think that this is wrong. You *can* learn from a book, in fact everyone who has learned any martial art that only survives in a manuscript or book has done just this. However, you don't do it if there's a choice. Having a competent instructor helps you to avoid the many possible pitfalls of analysing historical fencing treatises. This of course raises another problem. There are many groups and instructors out there. It can be almost impossible for the beginning student to work out which instructors are likely to help them progress in their understanding of the art. Interestingly, personal brilliance as a fencer is well down the list of what to look for in a good teacher. Brilliant fencers *may* be brilliant teachers, but commonly they have little patience with those who experience more difficulty learning than they did. As Archibald Macgregor wrote in 1791, "Another erroneous opinion which prevails with many, and I am afraid the greater part is, that if their master be a great swordsman, he can teach them to be swordsmen also. But this likewise is an error. For a man may be a very good swordsman, and yet not be enabled to communicate his art to others; on the contrary, a person may be but a very indifferent swordsman, nevertheless give good directions."[1]

Start by looking at the character of the teacher. Look for signs of impatience, a lack of humility and worst of all, for a bully. Avoid these people like the plague. The teacher you want is the one who is patient, humble and confident (but not overconfident). The good fencing instructor should be encyclopedic in his knowledge, but willing to admit that he does not know everything or that he may be mistaken.

Now look at how the instructor fences. It doesn't matter if he or she is old or slow or lacks the killer instinct. Are they technically excellent? Do they draw students into the fight and lift them or push them out and crush them? Do they stop and explain why they were able to make a hit and how the student might avoid being hit in the future?

It can also help to look at the instructor's public profile. Is the instructor well known? What does the rest of the community think of him or her? Is he or she invited to teach at major community events, or do they keep to themselves? A willingness to join the community, especially for the instructor to allow their students to train with other instructors, is a good sign. Conversely, any instructors who keep their students away from community events or who object to them learning from other instructors are to be avoided. Such people clearly fear that their students might question them, or even leave them if exposed to the broader community of scholars and instructors. This is not the sort of person you want teaching you.

The western martial arts field is one in which constant research is taking place into old fencing systems. Nobody knows everything about one historical system, let alone all of them. Therefore a very important thing to look for in any teacher is the willingness to change his teachings. This is truer, the older the system they are teaching you. Some people want certainty. You won't get it in historical martial arts. Expect your teacher to come in every few months and say, "you know how we were doing x like this? Well, after more research I now think we should do it more like this." This is a good sign. The bad instructor won't do this. This doesn't mean that they don't make mistakes in interpretation. They do. It's just that the bad instructor will either introduce changes by stealth, perhaps claiming that they'd done things that way all along and you haven't learned correctly, or worse, by simply not changing at all. Again, such people are to be avoided like the plague.

Probably above all else, can an instructor teach? Can he or she stand in front of a group class and explain principles and techniques so that you can understand them and do them? Can he or she show a movement to a class and get them to repeat it without error, or teach an individual lesson to a student with no natural aptitude for fencing (and in our experience even people with no natural aptitude can become fine fencers, given a patient and competent instructor)? If an instructor can't teach then he or she is about as useful as an ashtray on a motorbike.

The authors could mention many very fine instructors who we have had the great pleasure of working with, but inevitably we would forget someone. Instead let us list a few of the organisations that we are affiliated with. Firstly, the second author is the current Chairman of the Australian Historical Swordplay Federation, http://www.aushistsswordplayfed.org, a federation of all historical western swordsmanship groups in Australia. The second author is also an Acknowledged Instructor and Master at Arms candidate with the International Master at Arms Federation, http://www.scherma-tradionzale.org, an organization set up by professionally trained fencing masters who teach historical fencing, to train candidates to the internationally accepted standard for a professional fencing teacher (albeit with different weapons and in different styles than the ones used in the traditional fencing master's training).

There are many fine instructors out there. We hope that we have given you some insight into how to identify the good from those who, while trying hard, just aren't up to scratch and the fortunately very few out-and-out charlatans. Finding a good instructor is hard enough. Finding a good instructor for the I.33 system is harder. There are a few people out there studying I.33. The one person studying I.33 who we have had some contact with is Guy Windsor in Finland. He is the chief instructor of the School of European Swordsmanship in Helsinki. The school's website is http://www.swordschool.com. Guy has independently come to many of the same conclusions as the authors.

Other people we know of studying I.33 are (arranged alphabetically):

Martin Austwick,
The Company for Historical Combat
Robert Holland
Schola Saint George
John Jordan
Rocky Mountain Historical Combat Guild
Andrea Lupo Sinclair, *FISAS*
Dave Rawlings, *Boar's Tooth*

Any experienced fencer should be able to work from this book with a partner or a class and learn I.33. If you want to study I.33 and don't have an experienced instructor, you can always arrange a seminar with one of the authors (contact us through http://www.stoccata.org). This will kick-start your program of study, which coupled with this book, should allow you to faithfully re-create the system and achieve rapid results. Good Luck.

- NOTES -

[1] Archibald Macgregor, *Macgregor's Lecture on the Art of Defence*, 1791, p. 47

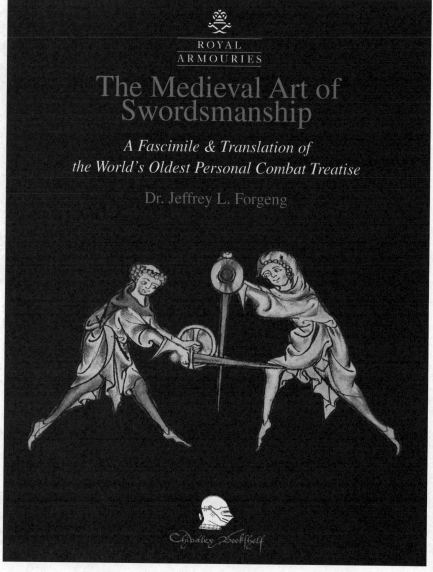